OFF~STAGI

Sketches from the English Teaching

Students' Book

Doug Case and Ken Wilson

Photographs by Richard Gibb

HEB

HEINEMANN

Heinemann International Publishing
a division of Heinemann Educational Books Ltd

Halley Court, Jordan Hill, Oxford OX2 8EJ
OXFORD   LONDON   EDINBURGH
MELBOURNE   SYDNEY   AUCKLAND
SINGAPORE   MADRID   IBADAN
NAIROBI   GABORONE   HARARE
KINGSTON   PORTSMOUTH (NH)

ISBN 0 435 28032 5
(Teachers' Book ISBN 0 435 28033 3)
(Cassettes ISBN 0 435 28035 X)

Text set in 10/11½ pt VIP Sabon, printed and bound in Great Britain
by Butler & Tanner Ltd, Frome and London

ACKNOWLEDGEMENTS

We would like to thank BBC English by Radio and Television for permission to reproduce the 'Ticket Inspector' sketch, which was originally written by Doug Case for the radio series 'Let's Speak English', and then adapted for the ETT's stage show. Information in the Customs Notice Number 1 (*The Customs Officer*) is reproduced with the permission of the Controller of Her Majesty's Stationery Office. This information is only correct at the time of printing and is subject to alteration. The extract from the Highway Code (*Gerry Brown's Driving Test*) is also with the permission of HMSO.

For information about the activities of the ETT, please write to:
The English Teaching Theatre, 40 Shaftesbury Avenue, London W1V 8HJ

We would also like to express our thanks to these people:
– to John Haycraft, for having the original idea for the ETT, and for constant support and encouragement ever since;
– to Jeremy Harrison and Piers Plowright, who first gave the show a style and identity;
– to all the members of the ETT, past and present, particularly to those who performed the sketches in this book with us during the 1974–78 tours: John Colclough, Susanne Elliott, Lawrence Fitzgerald, Kieran Fogarty, Bernard Fox, Roy Garner, Judy Garton-Sprenger, Sheila Hanley, Hazel Imbert, David Lochner, Magee, Coralyn Sheldon, Russ Shipton, Terry Tomscha and Hugh Trethowan;
– to all the organizations who have helped us with our tours, particularly International House, the British Council, BBC English by Radio and Television, the British Tourist Authority, British Airways, Air France and the Flemish Association of Teachers of EFL;
– and most of all, to all the teachers and students who have been our audiences, organizers and hosts, for their help, kindness, hospitality and enthusiasm.

Doug Case
Ken Wilson
July 1978

Contents

Introduction

The sketches in this book are taken from shows performed by the English Teaching Theatre. We hope you will enjoy listening to them, reading them and re-enacting them yourselves.

The ETT is a unique kind of theatre. It began in 1969 at International House, London, when the director, John Haycraft, said to one of his teachers, Jeremy Harrison: 'Why don't we have a theatre specially for students of English?' For several years there were summer seasons in London, and since 1974 the ETT has been a permanent theatre-group. Its members are teachers, actors and musicians, who spend eight months of each year on tour, performing in schools, teacher-training colleges, universities and theatres all over the world. Every year, more than 250 performances are given, and the show is seen on stage by more than 75,000 people – and on TV by many more.

The sketches in this book have been chosen from those performed in the ETT's shows between 1974 and 1978. They are accompanied by:

 * Questions   * Reading and writing exercises   * Discussion topics   * Word puzzles

and – very importantly – 'Communicating' and 'In your own words' exercises. These are important because (as John Haycraft said when talking about the beginnings of the ETT) 'English is not just words, structures and idioms; it is a lively, dramatic and versatile means of communication.'
We hope you enjoy the sketches in 'Off-stage!' – and that we may see you 'on stage' with the ETT one day.

1

The Ticket Inspector

SCENE	A compartment on a train
CHARACTERS	A passenger on a train
	A ticket inspector
	A steward and a waiter

I   *The passenger is sitting in a compartment on a train. He is reading a newspaper. The steward opens the door.*

STEWARD	Coffee!
PASSENGER	No, thanks.

The passenger closes the door, and continues reading. The waiter opens the door.

WAITER	Seats for dinner!
PASSENGER	No, thanks.

The passenger closes the door again, and continues reading. The ticket inspector opens the door.

INSPECTOR	Tickets!

PASSENGER	No, thanks.
INSPECTOR	Pardon?
PASSENGER	I don't want a ticket, thank you.
INSPECTOR	I'm not *selling* tickets, sir.
PASSENGER	No?
INSPECTOR	No. I want to *see your* ticket.
PASSENGER	Oh, I haven't got a ticket.
INSPECTOR	You haven't got a ticket?
PASSENGER	No. I never buy a ticket.
INSPECTOR	Why not?
PASSENGER	Well, they *are* very expensive, you know.
INSPECTOR	Sir, you're travelling on a train. When people travel on a train, they always buy a ticket.
PASSENGER	Er –
INSPECTOR	And *this* is a first-class compartment.
PASSENGER	Yes, it *is* very nice, isn't it?
INSPECTOR	No, sir. I mean: This is a *first-class* compartment. When people travel in a first-class compartment, they always buy a first-class ticket.
	They look at each other for a moment.
PASSENGER	No, they don't.
INSPECTOR	What?
PASSENGER	A lot of people don't buy tickets. The Queen doesn't buy a ticket, does she? Eh? Eh?
INSPECTOR	No, sir, but *she's* a famous person.
PASSENGER	And what about you? Where's yours?
INSPECTOR	Mine?
PASSENGER	Yes, yours. Your ticket. Have *you* got a ticket?
INSPECTOR	Me, sir?
PASSENGER	Yes, you.

II

	INSPECTOR	No, I haven't got a ticket.
	PASSENGER	Ooh – are you a famous person?
	INSPECTOR	(*Flattered:*) Famous? Well, not very – (*Back to normal:*) Sir, I am a ticket inspector. I inspect tickets. Are you going to show me your ticket?
	PASSENGER	No, I haven't got a ticket.
	INSPECTOR	I see.

III

The ticket inspector puts his hand into his pocket.

	PASSENGER	What are you going to do?
	INSPECTOR	I'm going to write your name in my book.
	PASSENGER	Oh.
	INSPECTOR	What is your name, sir?
	PASSENGER	Mickey Mouse.

The inspector begins to write.

	INSPECTOR	Mickey –
	PASSENGER	– Mouse. M-O-U-S-E.

The inspector stops writing.

	INSPECTOR	Your *name*, sir?
	PASSENGER	Karl Marx? William Shakespeare? Charles Dickens?

IV

	INSPECTOR	I see, sir. Well, if you're not going to tell me your name, please leave the train.
	PASSENGER	Pardon?
	INSPECTOR	Leave the train.
	PASSENGER	I can't.
	INSPECTOR	You can't what?
	PASSENGER	I can't leave the train.
	INSPECTOR	Why not?
	PASSENGER	It's moving.
	INSPECTOR	Not *now*, sir. At the next station.
	PASSENGER	Oh.
	INSPECTOR	It's in the book, sir. When you travel by train, you buy a ticket, and if you don't buy a ticket, you –
	PASSENGER } INSPECTOR }	– leave the train.
	INSPECTOR	Here we are, sir. We're coming to a station. Please leave the train now.
	PASSENGER	Now?
	INSPECTOR	Yes, sir. I'm sorry, but –
	PASSENGER	Oh, that's O.K.
	INSPECTOR	– it's in the book, and – What did you say?
	PASSENGER	I said: 'That's O.K.'
	INSPECTOR	O.K.?
	PASSENGER	Yes, this is my station. Goodbye.

The passenger leaves the train.

Questions

I
1. Did the passenger want coffee?
2. Did he have a ticket?
3. Was it a first or second-class compartment?

II
4. Why did the passenger mention the Queen?
5. Why did the ticket inspector say 'Mine'?

III
6. What was the passenger's name?
7. Why did the ticket inspector want to write down the passenger's name?

IV
8. Did the passenger buy a ticket?
9. Why did he leave the train?
10. Who was happier at the end?

True or False?

Read this text about the sketch. Say which of the sentences are *true* and which are *false*. If a sentence is false, say why.

> The passenger was watching the countryside through the train window, when the steward came into the compartment. He had some coffee, but did not go to the dining-car for dinner. He was travelling in a first-class compartment, but he did not have a first-class ticket. He only had a second-class ticket. He told the ticket inspector that he was a famous person, and so he never bought a ticket. The ticket inspector wrote his name in his book, and told him to leave the train. At the next station, the passenger got off the train, very angry.

Word Puzzle

When all the vertical columns are filled, the letters in the box will spell a word – a part of a train. All the words are in the sketch on pp. 4–6.

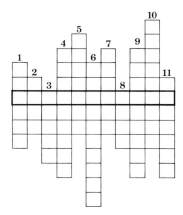

1. When you travel on a train, you must buy a . . . .
2. The ticket inspector wanted to write the man's name in his . . . .
3. The man said his surname was . . . .
4. Someone who inspects tickets is a ticket . . . .
5. When the . . . . came into the compartment, the man said he didn't want any coffee.
6. The man was sitting in a . . . . compartment.
7. The . . . . told the man about the seats for dinner.
8. The second surname the man gave was . . . .

9 The man didn't buy a ticket, because they were very . . . .
10 The . . . . left the train very happily.
11 He was happy because he got off at his . . . .

Communicating

1 Accepting and Refusing Offers

In the sketch, the passenger refused coffee and dinner, saying 'No, thanks'. In pairs, practise accepting and refusing offers. Use expressions from this table:

A:	Coffee? Tea? Do you want some beer? Would you like some cider?	B:	Yes, please. Yes, please. I'd love some. ------------------------------------ No, thanks./No, thank you. Not just now, thanks.

2 Giving Personal Details (Spelling)

Look at these lines from the sketch:

Ticket inspector	: What is your name, sir?
Passenger	: Mickey Mouse.
Ticket inspector	: Mickey –
Passenger	: – Mouse. M-O-U-S-E.

Practise in pairs. One person is a ticket inspector, policeman or other official, asking for the other person's name and address. The other person should give a name and address (real or invented) and spell it. The official should write it down.

In Your Own Words

Re-enact the sketch in your own words, without reading from the text. Do it in short sections. These words will remind you:

I
Coffee!
Tickets!
expensive
first-class

II
the Queen
Mine?
famous

III
name
book

IV
leave the train
station
O.K.

Writing

Regulations

The ticket inspector mentioned 'the book' – the book of regulations about railway passengers. In the book, there are regulations like this:

Passengers must have a valid ticket.

Write ten more regulations, using these patterns:

Passengers must (not) . . . . If passengers . . . ., they must . . . .

What Do You Think?

Jobs

In pairs, take the parts of (a) a ticket inspector, a traffic policeman or a park-keeper, (b) an interviewer.

If (a), decide on five good things and five bad things about your job. If (b), think of five questions to ask (a) about their job. Then ask and answer. Then discuss what makes a job interesting, and what your ideal job is.

2

Gussett and Rose

SCENE		A street
CHARACTERS		Two Englishmen: Albert Gussett and Harold Rose
I		*Two men pass in the street.*
	ROSE	Goodness me!
	GUSSETT	Well I never!
	ROSE	Herbert Bishop!
	GUSSETT	Arthur Trigwell!
	ROSE	No . . . actually my name's Harold Rose.
	GUSSETT	I'm Albert Gussett, as a matter of fact.
	ROSE	Albert Gussett. Of course.
	GUSSETT	And you're Harold Rose. Of course you are.
	ROSE	Well I never!
	GUSSETT	Goodness me!
		They hesitate for a moment.
	ROSE	Well, how are you, then?

GUSSETT		Fine, fine. How's Alice?
ROSE		Alice?
GUSSETT		Yes, Alice. Your wife's name's Alice, isn't it?
ROSE		No, no . . . Gloria, actually.
GUSSETT		Oh, yes. Gloria Trigwell.
ROSE		Er . . . Rose.
GUSSETT		Rose Trigwell?
ROSE		No. Gloria Rose.
GUSSETT		Gloria Rose. Of course. How is she?
ROSE		She's very well. How's . . . er . . .
GUSSETT		Doris?
ROSE		Yes, Doris, your wife. How is she?
GUSSETT		She's very well –
ROSE		Good, good.
GUSSETT		– but she isn't my wife.
ROSE		No?
GUSSETT		I'm not married.
ROSE		Oh.
GUSSETT		Doris is my sister.
ROSE		Oh, yes.

They hesitate again for a moment.

II		Well, it *is* a small world, isn't it, Herbert?
	GUSSETT	Albert.
	ROSE	Albert, yes. It seems like yesterday –
	GUSSETT	Yes, it certainly does . . .
	ROSE	– when we were at that awful school together.
	GUSSETT	School?
	ROSE	Yes. Doesn't time fly?
	GUSSETT	We weren't at school together.
	ROSE	Do you remember that awful English teacher with black teeth?
	GUSSETT	We *weren't* at school together.
	ROSE	Weren't we?
	GUSSETT	No, we were in the Army together.
	ROSE	We weren't.
	GUSSETT	Weren't we?
	ROSE	I was in the Navy.
	GUSSETT	Oh.

They hesitate again for a moment.

III	ROSE	Er . . . Albert, I mean *Herbert* –
	GUSSETT	No, no, Albert's my name.
	ROSE	Er, yes . . . Albert, how *do* we know each other?
	GUSSETT	I was just wondering about that myself, er . . .

ROSE	Harold.
GUSSETT	Yes, Harold. Are you an architect?
ROSE	Yes! Are *you* an architect?
GUSSETT	No, I'm a taxi-driver.
ROSE	Oh.
	They hesitate again.
GUSSETT	Are you interested in boxing?
ROSE	No, not at all.
GUSSETT	Ah.
ROSE	Do you go to the theatre?
GUSSETT	I went once – about twenty years go.
ROSE	I see.
GUSSETT	Do you take your holidays in Brighton?
ROSE	No, never.
GUSSETT	Mmm.
ROSE	Do you play golf?
GUSSETT	No, I don't.
ROSE	Well, that's not it then.
	They hesitate again.
IV	Do you know, Albert, I don't think we've met before.
GUSSETT	No, you're right. We haven't.
ROSE	Well, er . . . I'm Harold Rose.
GUSSETT	And I'm Albert Gussett.
ROSE	How do you do?
GUSSETT	How do you do?
	They shake hands.

Questions

I   1 How did the two men feel when they met each other?
   2 Who are Gloria and Doris?
II 3 Did the two men go to the same school?
   4 Who had been in the Army and who had been in the Navy?
III 5 What was Albert Gussett's job?
   6 Did both men like playing golf?
IV 7 Did they have anything in common?
   8 Was this their first meeting?

Read and Re-tell

Read the story, and then re-tell it.

> A young man went to work for the British diplomatic service in India. Twenty years later, he returned to England. Everything was completely different. After a few days, he was invited to go to a party. He arrived, feeling rather lost and lonely. Suddenly, he saw a face that he recognized – a lady he used to know when he was younger. He rushed across the room.
>
> 'Hello, how are you?' he said, smiling.
>
> The lady looked at him blankly.
>
> 'I've just come back from India,' he said, still smiling. 'Been there twenty years.'
>
> 'Have you?' said the lady, puzzled.
>
> 'Yes,' said the man, beginning to feel rather uncomfortable. 'Er . . . how's your sister, by the way?'
>
> 'Oh, she's very well,' said the lady, surprised. 'She's still the Queen.'

Word Puzzle

There are a lot of *names* in the sketch, including a few wrong ones! Read the sketch again, fill in the names, and find the word in the box. Be careful – Number 5 is different from the others.

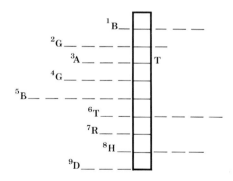

Communicating

1 Meeting by Accident

Gussett and Rose said:

| Goodness me! |
| Well I never! |

You can practise with:

| What a surprise to see you! |
| I can't believe it! |
| What on earth are you doing here? |
| I wasn't expecting to see *you* here! |

Gussett and Rose said:

> Are you interested in boxing?
> – No, not at all.
> Do you take your holidays in Brighton?
> – No, never.

They did not find any common interests. But if you do have common interests, you can show it like this:

Do you like skiing?	Yes, quite a lot. Yes, I love it. Yes, I'm very keen on skiing.

Have you been to Paris?	Yes, lots of times. Yes, once or twice. I went last year for the first time.

If not, then:

Do you like	collecting stamps? climbing mountains? Shakespeare? classical music?	No, not much. Not very much. Not really. No, not at all. Not any more. Not these days.

In Your Own Words
Re-enact the sketch in your own words, without reading from the text. Do it in short sections. These words will remind you:

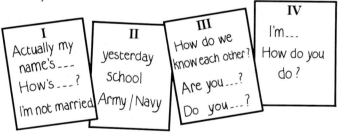

Writing

Notes for a Biography
Read the sketch very carefully, and write down everything you can find out about Albert Gussett and Harold Rose.
Make *notes* about their jobs, families and hobbies. Then use your notes to write a biography of each man.

What do You Think?

Strangers
Gussett and Rose were very uncomfortable when they realized that they were strangers. It is said that the English never speak to strangers on buses, in trains, in cafés, etc. Do you think this is a bad thing? Do you talk to strangers when you have the chance? Where?

3
Yoga for Beginners

SCENE	A room in the woman's house
CHARACTERS	A woman who is studying yoga The voice on a cassette

I WOMAN   Right.

She puts her cassette-player on a table, and checks it.

Play. Stop. Fast forward. Stop. Rewind. Stop. Yes, that's O.K. Now . . .

She finds the cassette.

. . . ah, yes, here it is. 'Yoga for Beginners'. Good.

She puts the cassette into the cassette-player.

Now. Play.

She starts the cassette.

VOICE   'Yoga for Beginners'. Lesson 1, Part 1, Unit 1, Section 1, Paragraph 1: *One*. Do this first exercise on the floor. *Sit* on the floor.

The woman follows the instructions.

Cross your legs and straighten your back. Now relax. Relax. Every part of your body must *relax*.

The woman falls over.

Hmm. Now sit up again. Straighten your back and relax. But keep your back straight.

The woman does this.

II   Good. Lesson 1, Part 1, Unit 1, Section 1, Paragraph 1: *Two.* Now touch your right knee –

WOMAN	Oh, that's easy.

The woman touches her right knee.

VOICE	– with your head. But keep your back straight.
WOMAN	Oh. (*Doing it:*) Ow . . . ooh!
VOICE	Good. Now put your *right* hand under your *left* knee, and hold your *right* foot.
WOMAN	Right hand . . . left knee . . . right foot. I've done that.
VOICE	Good. Now, put your *left* hand under your *right* knee, and hold your *left* foot.
WOMAN	Left hand . . . right knee . . . left foot. Yes, I've done that.
VOICE	And keep your back straight.
WOMAN	Oh.

She tries to do this, and falls over again.

Aaaargh!

VOICE	Now sit up again and relax. Good. Lesson 1, Part 1, Unit 1, Section 1, Paragraph 1: *Three.* Put your *right* hand under your *right* knee, and hold your *right* foot.
WOMAN	Oh, dear. Right hand . . . right knee . . . right foot. Yes, I've done that.
VOICE	Good. Now put your *left* hand under your *left* knee, and hold your *left* foot.

The woman tries to do this.

WOMAN	I can't do it.
VOICE	Now, come along. Put your *left* hand under your *left* knee, and hold your *left* foot.

The woman tries again.

WOMAN	I can't do it.

She stands up and walks across to the table.

III   No more yoga for me.

VOICE	Don't touch that button!
WOMAN	What?!
VOICE	Don't touch that button!
WOMAN	What do you mean: 'Don't touch that button'?
VOICE	Don't touch it.
WOMAN	Don't talk to me like that.
VOICE	Don't touch that button . . . *please.*
WOMAN	That's better.

VOICE	Let's try again.
WOMAN	It's too difficult.
VOICE	No, it isn't. Let's try again.
WOMAN	Why?
VOICE	Well, because yoga is good for you.
WOMAN	Good for you?
VOICE	Yes. Everybody does it: doctors do it . . .
WOMAN	(*Not interested:*) Really?
VOICE	. . . university professors do it . . .
WOMAN	(*Not interested:*) Really?
VOICE	. . . and famous actresses and film stars do it.
WOMAN	(*Interested:*) Really? Oh, well . . . O.K.

She sits on the floor again.

IV

Now . . . right hand under right knee . . . hold right foot. Yes, I've done that.

VOICE	Good. Now put your *left* hand under your *left* knee, and hold your *left* foot.
WOMAN	Left hand . . . left knee . . . left foot. I've done it!

VOICE	Good. That position is Position One. Now: Instructions for getting *out* of Position One. Getting out of Position One is not very difficult. But you must follow the instructions very carefully.

The tape begins to slow down.

First . . . take . . . your . . . left . . . hand . . .

WOMAN	Oh, no! The batteries! Um . . . quick! Hurry up! . . . Help! Help!

Questions

I   1   Was the woman standing up for the first exercise?
      2   Was the first exercise easy?
II   3   Did the woman do the second exercise?
      4   What happened at the end of the second exercise?
      5   Why did the woman want to stop the lesson?
III 6   Did the cassette say anything unusual?
      7   What kind of people did the cassette mention?
      8   Why did the woman continue the lesson?
IV 9   What was wrong with the cassette-player?
    10 Why did the woman shout 'Help!'?

Where Could You Read This?

Read these instructions and say where they come from.

1
> Place in boiling water.
> Boil for ten minutes.
> Serve hot.

2
> Write in ink.
> Use BLOCK CAPITALS.
> Put the date and your signature at the bottom.

3
> Dissolve one tablet in a little water.
> Repeat the dose every three hours.
> Maximum: Eight doses in 24 hours.

4
> Do not feed the animals.
> Keep away from the bars.

5
> Lift receiver and wait for dialling tone.
> Dial number.
> Insert coin or coins.
> (Repeat for more time.)

Word Puzzle

Look at this diagram of a cassette recorder. What are the numbered parts? Write the words in the horizontal boxes. The letters in the vertical box will spell a word.

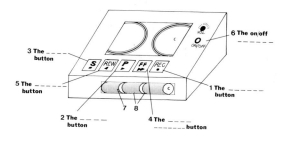

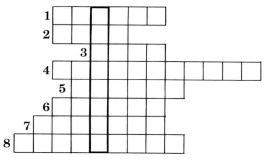

18

Communicating

1 Giving and Following Instructions

The cassette gave the woman instructions. For example:

> Put your right hand under your right knee, and hold your right foot.

The woman followed the instructions. For example:

> Right hand . . . right knee . . . right foot.
> Yes, I've done that.

Practise in pairs, giving and following instructions in the same way. Use these instructions from p. 78:

> Lift receiver and wait for dialling tone.
> Dial number.
> Insert coin or coins. (Repeat for more time.)

2 Persuading

The cassette persuaded the woman to continue with yoga:

> – Why?
> – Well, because yoga is good for you. . . . Everybody does it: doctors do it . . . university professors do it . . . and famous actresses and film stars do it.

Listen to that part of the sketch again. Then make similar dialogues about:

riding a bicycle / jogging / meditation

You can use these phrases:

It'll make you	healthy. successful, etc.
If you don't . . .	you'll be . . . you won't be . . .

In Your Own Words

Re-enact the sketch in your own words, without reading from the text. Do it in short sections. These words will remind you:

I
Lesson 1.
on the floor
relax

II
right hand
left knee
right foot

III
No more
button
try again
good for you

IV
Position 1
instructions
batteries

Writing

Instructions in a Handbook
This is the first page of the woman's 'Yoga for Beginners' handbook:

YOGA FOR BEGINNERS: LESSON 1
Part 1
Unit 1
Section 1
Paragraph 1

1: Do this first exercise on the floor. *Sit* on the floor. Cross your legs and straighten your back. Now relax. Every part of your body must relax. Now sit up again. Straighten your back and relax . . . but keep your back straight.
2: . . . .
3: . . . .
4: . . . .

Listen to the sketch again, and write exercises 2 and 3. Then add a fourth exercise of your own.

What Do You Think?

Learning
What is the best way to learn: to learn a language, for example?
In a class with a teacher? At home with a cassette? By watching TV? With a loudspeaker under your pillow while you sleep?

4

Mr Jones

SCENE	An office, at four o'clock one afternoon
CHARACTERS	A girl
	Mr Charles Jones
	'Mr Jones' No. 2
	'Mr Jones' No. 3

I

Mr Jones goes into an office.

MR JONES	Good afternoon.
GIRL	Good afternoon.
MR JONES	My name's Jones. Charles Jones. I come from Wales, from Cardiff. I saw an advertisement in the newspaper. It said: 'Charles Jones. Money. Four o'clock. Tuesday afternoon.' And it gave this address.
GIRL	Ah yes. Wait in here please, Mr Jones.

She takes Mr Jones into another office.

MR JONES	Thank you.
GIRL	With these two gentlemen.
MR JONES	Oh, thank you.
	The girl goes out.
MR JONES	Good afternoon.
MR JONES 2	Good afternoon.
MR JONES	Good afternoon.
MR JONES 3	Good afternoon.
MR JONES	Nice day, isn't it?
MR JONES 2	Yes.
MR JONES 3	Yes, it is.

II

	The girl comes in.
GIRL	Now – Mr Jones?
MR JONES	
MR JONES 2	} Yes?
MR JONES 3	
GIRL	Mr *Jones*.
MR JONES	
MR JONES 2	} Yes?
MR JONES 3	
GIRL	Which one of you is Mr Jones?
MR JONES	I am.
MR JONES 2	So am I.
MR JONES 3	So am I.
MR JONES	No, *my* name's Jones.
MR JONES 2	So's mine.
MR JONES 3	So's mine.
GIRL	I want to speak to Mr *Charles* Jones.
MR JONES	Charles Jones! That's me!
MR JONES 2	No, *I'm* Charles Jones.
MR JONES 3	That's my name, too!
GIRL	Charles *Edward* Jones.
MR JONES	Yes! My name is Charles Edward Jones.
MR JONES 3	So's mine.
MR JONES 2	Mine is, too!
GIRL	I want to speak to Mr Charles Edward Jones from Cardiff.
MR JONES	That's right. *I* come from Cardiff.
MR JONES 2	*(In a Welsh accent:)* So do I.
MR JONES 3	So do I.
MR JONES	You don't! You haven't got a Welsh accent.
MR JONES 3	I know. I went to a good school.
GIRL	The Mr Jones I want to see has got three children.
MR JONES	Yes, that's me! I've got three children.

MR JONES 3		So have I.
		The other man hesitates.
GIRL		What about you?
MR JONES 2		I've got three children.
MR JONES		You haven't! What are they called?
MR JONES 2		What are *yours* called?
MR JONES		Alan, Michael and David.
MR JONES 2		So are mine.
MR JONES 3		What a coincidence! So are mine.
GIRL		So you *all* say you're Mr Jones?
MR JONES	⎫	
MR JONES 2	⎬	Yes.
MR JONES 3	⎭	
GIRL		And you *all* saw the advertisement in the newspaper.
MR JONES	⎫	
MR JONES 2	⎬	Yes.
MR JONES 3	⎭	
GIRL		(*Very seriously:*) Well, Mr Charles Edward Jones, who lives in Cardiff, and has three children, hasn't paid any tax for the last five years. He must pay the government *five thousand pounds*.

III

MR JONES 2		Er . . . actually, my name *isn't* Jones.
MR JONES 3		Nor is mine, and I don't live in Cardiff, either.
MR JONES 2		Nor do I. I live in . . . Edinburgh, as a matter of fact. I didn't understand the advertisement.
MR JONES 3		Nor did I. I didn't realize it meant Charles *Edward* Jones.
MR JONES 2		Nor did I. My name isn't Charles *Edward* Jones.
MR JONES 3		Nor is mine. *He's* the man you're looking for.
MR JONES		Oh dear.
MR JONES 2		Yes, of course he is! Sorry to have troubled you. Goodbye.
MR JONES 3		Yes, sorry to have troubled you. Goodbye.
		The two men leave.

IV

GIRL		So you're Mr Jones.
MR JONES		Yes.
GIRL		Congratulations.
MR JONES		Eh?
GIRL		You're a rich man.
MR JONES		I'm not!
GIRL		Yes, you are. You've got a lot of money!
MR JONES		I haven't. I can't pay that tax.
GIRL		There isn't any tax!
MR JONES		I haven't got – No tax?
GIRL		No. That was just a story. I had to find the *real* Mr Jones.
MR JONES		Why?
GIRL		Because the real Mr Jones is a very rich man.

MR JONES	I don't understand.
GIRL	Mr Jones – Charlie – Your great-uncle Max died last week.
MR JONES	Oh, no . . .
GIRL	And his money goes to you!
MR JONES	To me? But great-uncle Max was a millionaire!
GIRL	That's right.
MR JONES	So now *I'm* a millionaire?
GIRL	Er . . . no.
MR JONES	Oh.
GIRL	You're *half* a millionaire.
MR JONES	Half a millionaire? Which half? The top half or the bottom half?
GIRL	No, no, no. You share the money with one other relation.
MR JONES	Half a millionaire! Who do I share the money with?
GIRL	Me!
MR JONES	You?
GIRL	Yes, I'm your cousin Jane.
MR JONES	Cousin Jane? Really? *You've* grown up!
GIRL	So have you.
MR JONES	And now you're half a millionaire.
GIRL	And so are you! Let's go out and celebrate.
MR JONES	Good idea! Let's go out and celebrate! Come on!
	He opens the door.
	Oh . . . er . . . Jane?
GIRL	Yes?
MR JONES	Have you got enough money for the bus fare?

Questions

I   1   What did the advertisement in the newspaper say?
      2   Where was Mr Jones from?
II   3   What was Mr Jones' full name?
      4   How many children did he have?
      5   What were Mr Jones' children called?
      6   How did the girl explain the advertisement?
III 7   Why did the two men leave?
IV 8   Why did the girl congratulate Mr Jones?
      9   Why did she tell the story about the tax?
    10 What did Mr Jones and Jane decide to do?

Advertisements: Read and Explain

Mr Jones read this advertisement in the personal column of a newspaper:

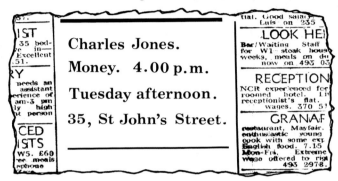

These are some more advertisements from the same column. What do they mean?

1   Paul. Desperate. Please ring. Annette.

2   Lost: Diamond necklace. Big reward. Ring 0215-996.

3   Wanted: Anything old. Good prices. Box 27.

4   Lonely? Meet new friends at Tony's. Tuesdays, 8.00 p.m.

5   Young man, 23, needs money. Anything legal considered. Box 28.

Word Puzzle

Solve the puzzle below, and you'll find the word which describes a man like Mr Jones. It will appear in the diagonal squares.

No. 1 is where Mr Jones comes from.
No. 2 is where he saw the advertisement.
No. 3 describes his great-uncle Max.
No. 4 is the day he had to go to the office.
No. 5 is his first name.
Nos. 6, 7 and 8 are the names of his children.

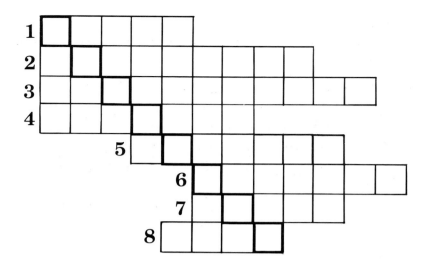

Communicating

1 Misunderstandings

In the sketch, the two men said that they did not understand the advertisement. They were pretending, but sometimes you really need to show that you didn't understand something, for example, if you want to return something to a shop, or change a ticket after you've bought it. In this situation, you could say:

> I didn't realize what sort it was.
> I thought it was (a return ticket/a cotton shirt).
> I didn't mean to buy one of these.

Practise in pairs:
– taking a shirt back to a shop
– taking a ticket back to a ticket office
– taking a ticket back to a theatre

For example:
'Good morning . . .
I bought this shirt here (yesterday) . . .
I thought it was a . . .
I didn't realize it was a . . .
I'd like to exchange it for a . . .' etc.

2 Apologizing

In the sketch, the two men said:

> 'Sorry to have troubled you.'

as they left.
Practise apologizing like that. In pairs, make dialogues like this:

A : Good morning. Can I help you?
B : Yes. I'd like to buy *a hat*.
A : I'm sorry. We don't sell *hats*. This is *a bookshop*.
B : Is it really? Sorry to have troubled you. Goodbye.
A : Goodbye.

Put your own words for those in italics.

In Your Own Words

Re-enact the sketch in your own words, without reading from the text. Do it in short sections. These words will remind you:

Writing

A Dialogue

When Mr Jones came home, his wife wanted to know what had happened. This is what Mrs Jones said. What did Mr Jones say?

Mrs Jones	Well, dear – good news or bad?
Mr Jones	. . . .
Mrs Jones	What do you mean: 'good *and* bad'?
Mr Jones	. . . .
Mrs Jones	Great-uncle Max? Oh, how sad! What's the *good* news?
Mr Jones	. . . .
Mrs Jones	What – *all* his money?
Mr Jones	. . . .
Mrs Jones	But he was a millionaire, wasn't he?
Mr Jones	. . . .
Mrs Jones	Half a million pounds! Well, we've got to celebrate!
Mr Jones	. . . .
Mrs Jones	What do you mean – you've already celebrated?
Mr Jones	. . . .
Mrs Jones	Jane? Who's Jane?
Mr Jones	. . . .
Mrs Jones	I see. So that's why you're so late.

What Do You Think?

Money

Charles Jones is a lucky man – he's got half a million pounds to spend. He won't have any problems for the rest of his life. On the other hand, perhaps his problems are just beginning. What do you think?

5

The Customs Officer

SCENE	The customs hall at an airport or port in England
CHARACTERS	A customs officer
	Vladimir Strogonov

1 OFFICER   Good morning, sir.

STROGONOV   Good morning.

OFFICER   Welcome to England.

STROGONOV   Thank you.

OFFICER   Are you staying long?

STROGONOV   Yes. Er . . . no. Perhaps. I'm not sure.

OFFICER   I see. Could I see your passport, please?

STROGONOV   Yes. Here you are.

OFFICER   Thank you.

Strogonov gives the customs officer a passport. (Reading from the passport:) Mrs Elizabeth Robinson?

STROGONOV   Oh, sorry. Try this one.

He gives the customs officer another passport.

	OFFICER	This is very strange, sir. Why have you got *two* passports?
	STROGONOV	Well, I travel a lot.
	OFFICER	I see. Hmm . . . (*Reading from the passport:*) Name: Vladimir Strogonov.
	STROGONOV	*Strogo*nov.
	OFFICER	Pardon?
	STROGONOV	*Strogo*nov. Vladimir *Strogo*nov.
	OFFICER	*Strogo*nov, yes. Nationality . . . Nationality: British?!
	STROGONOV	That's right.
	OFFICER	Vladimir Strogonov doesn't *sound* very British.
	STROGONOV	Doesn't it?
	OFFICER	No – and *you* don't *look* very British, either.
	STROGONOV	Don't I?
	OFFICER	No, you don't.
	STROGONOV	Oh.

II	OFFICER	Name, nationality . . . occupation. Occupation: Spy!?
	STROGONOV	What?
	OFFICER	It says here that you're a spy.
	STROGONOV	Let me see.
		He looks at the passport.
		Yes, it looks like 'Spy', doesn't it?
	OFFICER	Yes, it does.
	STROGONOV	It's a spelling mistake.
	OFFICER	A spelling mistake? What *is* your job then?
	STROGONOV	I'm a brush salesman.
	OFFICER	A brush salesman?
	STROGONOV	Yes. Would you like to buy a new toothbrush?
	OFFICER	No!
	STROGONOV	A paintbrush?
	OFFICER	No!
	STROGONOV	A hairbrush?
	OFFICER	No!! Now, you say your name is Vladimir Strogonov, and you say you're British. Your passport says you're a spy, and *you* say you're a brush salesman.
	STROGONOV	That's right.
	OFFICER	Well, it all looks very suspicious, doesn't it?
	STROGONOV	Yes, I suppose it does.

III	OFFICER	Now, have you got anything to declare?
	STROGONOV	Yes, I have.
	OFFICER	What?
	STROGONOV	I love my wife.
	OFFICER	I'm not interested in your wife.
	STROGONOV	I'm very pleased to hear it. I can assure you that my wife is not interested in *you* either.

OFFICER		Sir!! When I say: 'Have you got anything to declare?' I mean: 'Have you got any whisky? Have you got any cigarettes? Have you got any wine? Etcetera, etcetera.'
	STROGONOV	No. No 'etceteras' at all.
	OFFICER	Then what is *that*, in your pocket?
	STROGONOV	Where?
	OFFICER	*There!*

The customs officer takes a bottle from Mr Strogonov's pocket.

Ah, yes. Now *this* looks like a bottle of whisky to me.

	STROGONOV	Yes, it *looks* like a bottle of whisky – but it isn't.
	OFFICER	What is it, then?
	STROGONOV	It's a bottle of . . . perfume.
	OFFICER	I see. I think I'd better take it.

The customs officer puts the bottle in a drawer.

IV		Now – your case.
	STROGONOV	My case?
	OFFICER	Yes – on the table, please.
	STROGONOV	On the table?
	OFFICER	Yes.

Mr Strogonov puts his case on the table.

What's that noise?

	STROGONOV	What noise?
	OFFICER	That *ticking* noise. It's coming from your case.
	STROGONOV	Oh, *that* noise.
	OFFICER	Yes. It sounds like a clock. Is it a clock, Mr Strogonov? Or is it a bomb?
	STROGONOV	It's a brush.
	OFFICER	A brush?
	STROGONOV	Yes. It's a special new toothbrush with an alarm-clock attached to it.
	OFFICER	An alarm-clock?
	STROGONOV	Yes. It wakes you up when it's time to clean your teeth.
	OFFICER	I don't believe a word of it. Would you mind *opening* the case please, sir?
	STROGONOV	I can't.
	OFFICER	Why not?
	STROGONOV	It's locked.
	OFFICER	Well, *un*lock it.
	STROGONOV	I've lost the key.
	OFFICER	I see. (*He calls to another customs officer:*) George, bring me that hammer, would you? That's right – the large one.
	STROGONOV	What?! Hammer? No, no! It's not locked.

He opens the case.

There you are.

V	OFFICER	Thank you, sir. Aha! What is this?

He takes a toothbrush out of the case. There is an alarm-clock attached to it.

STROGONOV	You see – a toothbrush with an alarm-clock attached to it.
OFFICER	And what is this?
	He takes some dynamite out of the case. It is attached to the toothbrush and alarm-clock.
	It looks like dynamite.
STROGONOV	That's right.
OFFICER	Dynamite?!
STROGONOV	Yes.
OFFICER	What's it for?
STROGONOV	Well, if the alarm-clock doesn't work, it blows up. Boom!
OFFICER	Blows up?
STROGONOV	Yes. Some people can't wake up in the morning.
OFFICER	(*Ironically:*) Very interesting.
	The customs officer finds some papers in the case.
	And what are these papers?
STROGONOV	Oh, they're just information about brushes.
OFFICER	Let's have a look. These look like secret papers to me. You haven't come to England to sell these papers, have you, Mr Strogonov?
STROGONOV } OFFICER }	*Strog*onov.
OFFICER	Now come along, Mr Strogonov. Have you come to England to *sell* these secret papers?
STROGONOV	Well . . . as a matter of fact . . . yes, I have.
OFFICER	(*Very severely:*) I see. Well, in that case, Mr Strogonov . . . (*Suddenly very friendly:*) . . . welcome to England.
STROGONOV	Eh?
OFFICER	Welcome to England. There's a car waiting for you outside.
STROGONOV	Oh. Thank you very much.
OFFICER	Goodbye, sir.
STROGONOV	Goodbye.
	Mr Strogonov leaves.
OFFICER	Right. Who's next? Good morning, madam. Welcome to England . . .

Questions

I 1 What was wrong with Strogonov's first passport?
   2 Why was the customs officer surprised when he read 'British' in Strogonov's passport?
II 3 How did Strogonov explain the word 'Spy' in his passport?
    4 Do you think Strogonov was a brush salesman?
III 5 Why did the customs officer say: 'I'm not interested in your wife.'?
     6 Where did the customs officer see the bottle?
IV 7 What happened when Strogonov put his case on the table?
    8 How did Strogonov explain the noise?
    9 Was Strogonov's case locked?
   10 Did the customs officer use the hammer?
V 11 What was the dynamite for?
   12 Why was Strogonov surprised at the end?

Read and Explain

Look at the lists below. They show the duty-free allowances for EEC and non-EEC visitors to Britain.

EEC PASSPORT HOLDERS	NON-EEC PASSPORT HOLDERS
300 cigarettes	200 cigarettes
or	or
150 cigarillos	100 cigarillos
or	or
75 cigars	50 cigars
or	or
400 grammes of tobacco	250 grammes of tobacco
3 litres of table wine	2 litres of table wine
or	or
$1\frac{1}{2}$ litres of spirits	1 litre of spirits

Read the lists and then explain the regulations. Use expressions like:

	you're allowed to . . .
	you can . . .
If you're an EEC passport holder	– – – – – – – – – – – –
	you're not allowed to . . .
	you can't . . .
	you mustn't (etc.) . . .

Word Puzzle

Be careful: this is a TOP SECRET word puzzle!

1 2 3 4 5 6 7 8 1

⬜⬜⬜⬜⬜⬜⬜⬜⬜

If you answer the questions below, you'll find out which letters correspond to the numbers above – and you'll be able to fill in the word.

Strogonov had two of these.   3   7   2   2   3   5   –   –   2

⬜⬜⬜⬜⬜⬜⬜⬜⬜

What sort of papers did he have?

2	1	–	–	1	–

One of the brushes Strogonov offered to the customs officer was a . . . . . . (Be careful!)

3	7	4	6	–	–	–	–	2	–

Here is a final clue: No. 8 is the *middle* letter of the spy's *surname*.

When you have filled in the word in the top box, say what it means.

Communicating

1 Clearing up Misunderstandings

Listen again to the beginning of Part III of the sketch, where the customs officer asked: 'Have you got anything to declare?' When Strogonov misunderstood him, he explained. Practise that section of the sketch in pairs.

Then continue these dialogues:

A Have you seen my glasses anywhere?
B Yes.
A Where?
B You were wearing them yesterday.
. . . .
A Have you been to this country before?
B Yes.
A When?
B Yesterday.
. . . .

You can use these phrases to clear up the misunderstandings:

> No, you don't understand.
> No, what I meant was . . .
> I don't think you quite understand.
> That's not what I meant.

2 Showing Disbelief

Listen again to the way the customs officer showed that he did not believe the details in Strogonov's passport ('You say you're British' etc.). Listen to the tone of his voice.

Then look at the details below. A man is speaking to you on the telephone, and at the same time you are telling a friend what the man says about himself.

Name   : Albert Pickles
Occupation: Minister of Defence
Address   : Buckingham Palace
Salary   : £100,000 per year.

Begin: 'He *says* . . .'

In Your Own Words

Re-enact the sketch in your own words, without reading from the text. Do it in short sections.
These words will remind you:

I
passport
two passports
name
occupation

II
spy
brush salesman
suspicious

III
Anything to
declare?
bottle of
whisky

IV
case
noise
alarm-clock
locked

V
dynamite
secret papers
Welcome to
England

Writing

Filling in a Form

You have to write down the following information about a visitor to your country:

Name	....
Nationality	....
Date of birth	....
Date of arrival	....
Length of stay	....
Probable date of departure	....
Passport Number	....

Work in pairs, one student asking the questions and the other filling in the form.

What Do You Think?

Passports

Passports are a problem. They are easy to lose, and when they expire, you have to queue to get
a new one. Often the photograph doesn't look like you. It would be better if we didn't have
them. Do you agree?

6

The Dentist

SCENE	A dentist's waiting-room
CHARACTERS	Two patients: a man and a woman A 'dentist' The real dentist

The man and the woman are sitting in the waiting-room. The woman is calm, but the man is very nervous.

I	MAN	Um . . . is he good?
	WOMAN	Pardon?
	MAN	The dentist. Is he good?
	WOMAN	I don't know.

MAN	You don't know?
WOMAN	No. I haven't seen him before. He's new.
MAN	New!?
WOMAN	Yes. It's his first day.
MAN	Oh. . . . This is *my* first visit, you know.
WOMAN	Oh really?
MAN	It's the first time I've been here.
WOMAN	Oh.
MAN	Don't you understand? It's the first time I've been to the dentist in my life!
WOMAN	I see.
	The man looks at his watch.
MAN	He's late, isn't he?
WOMAN	Well, it *is* his first day.
MAN	Oh well, perhaps I won't wait. I can come back tomorrow . . . or the next day.
	They hear the dentist coming.
WOMAN	Ah, here he comes now.
MAN	(*Disappointed:*) Oh, good.

II

	The 'dentist' comes in, carrying a large bag.
'DENTIST'	Ah, good morning, good morning, good morning. Sorry I'm late. Now, who's first?
WOMAN	He was here first.
MAN	Oh no, after you.
WOMAN	No, no, you were before me.
MAN	No, no, ladies first.
'DENTIST'	Now, now, what seems to be the matter?
MAN	I've got a bad tooth.
WOMAN	So have I.
'DENTIST'	Well, I can do you both at the same time.
MAN WOMAN	Both at the same time?
'DENTIST'	Yes. I've got two pieces of string. Look!
WOMAN	String? To take out a tooth? Have you done that before?
'DENTIST'	Not on people, no. But I tried it this morning on the cat.
WOMAN	And was the cat all right?
'DENTIST'	Oh, yes! It got up, ran across the room, and jumped out of the window. And we live on the thirteenth floor.
WOMAN	The thirteenth floor?
'DENTIST'	Don't worry, the cat's not superstitious.
MAN	But dentists don't use *string* to take out teeth!
'DENTIST'	Don't they? What do you want, then?
MAN	Well, to begin with, I'd like an anaesthetic.
'DENTIST'	Oh, you'd like an anaesthetic, would you? Just a minute.

36

He takes a hammer out of his bag.

Ah, yes. Here we are.

WOMAN	What's that?
'DENTIST'	A hammer.
MAN	Is that the anaesthetic?
'DENTIST'	I'm not sure. It's the first time I've given an anaesthetic. Sit still.

He hits the man on the head, knocking him out.

MAN	Ow! Ohh!
'DENTIST'	Oh, it works!

He puts the hammer down.

III

Now, madam, what's the matter with you?

WOMAN	I've got a pain.
'DENTIST'	Where?
WOMAN	In my mouth.
'DENTIST'	Yes, I know it's in your mouth, but which tooth?
WOMAN	This one here.
'DENTIST'	Ah yes, a molar.
WOMAN	What are you going to do?
'DENTIST'	I'm going to take it out.
WOMAN	How?
'DENTIST'	I don't know.
WOMAN	You don't know?
'DENTIST'	No. This is the first time I've taken out a molar. In fact, it's the first time I've taken out a tooth.
WOMAN	The first time you've taken out a tooth!
'DENTIST'	Yes. This is a very important day for me – my first extraction. Now, where's that hammer?
WOMAN	Listen, I don't want the hammer and I don't want the string. I want you to take out my tooth with a pair of –
'DENTIST'	A pair of scissors?
WOMAN	No.
'DENTIST'	A pair of socks?
WOMAN	No.
'DENTIST'	A pair of trousers?
WOMAN	No.
'DENTIST'	Oh. Just a minute.

He looks inside his bag, and takes out a large pair of forceps.

These?

WOMAN	Yes, I suppose so.
'DENTIST'	Right then. Open your mouth.
WOMAN	But what about the anaesthetic?
'DENTIST'	Oh yes. Pass me the hammer.
WOMAN	I don't *want* the hammer! I want a *proper* anaesthetic. I want an injection.

'DENTIST'	An injection?	
WOMAN	Yes.	
'DENTIST'	Just a minute.	

He looks inside his bag again, and takes out a large syringe.

	Ah yes, this is for injections, isn't it? How does it work?
WOMAN	Well, you're the dentist. Don't *you* know?
'DENTIST'	No. It's the first time I've used one of these. Oh well, I'll have a try. Open your mouth.
WOMAN	Er, no . . . I don't think you really know . . . er . . . no, no, I'll come back another day. I –

IV

	The man wakes up.
MAN	Where am I? Hey, what are you doing?
'DENTIST'	I'll be with you in a moment, sir. Now, just sit still, madam . . .
MAN	No, stop that! You're absolutely crazy!
WOMAN	I agree. He's absolutely crazy, completely mad. Let's get out of here.
MAN	Oh yes, good idea.
'DENTIST'	So you don't want me to take out that molar?
WOMAN	Certainly not. (*To the man:*) Come on.
MAN	Yes. Good idea.
	The man and the woman leave.
'DENTIST'	Hmm, that worked very well.
	He puts his things into the bag, laughing to himself.
	'But dentists don't use *string* to take out teeth! – 'Oh, you'd like an anaesthetic, would you?'
	The real dentist arrives.
DENTIST	Oh, good morning. Sorry I'm late. It's my first day. It's the first time I've been here. Are you the only one?
'DENTIST'	Yes, there's just me.
DENTIST	Right. You can come straight in, then.
'DENTIST'	Oh, good. I hate having to wait.

Questions

I   1   What was the difference between the two patients?
    2   Did the man visit the dentist regularly?
    3   How did the man feel when the 'dentist' arrived?
II 4   Why did the 'dentist' say he could do both patients at the same time?
    5   What did he use for an anaesthetic?
    6   Did it work?
III 7   How many molars had the 'dentist' taken out?
    8   Did the woman want an anaesthetic?
IV 9   What did the man see when he woke up?
    10 Why was the real dentist late?

Wrong!

Correct the following statements.

1   The 'dentist' wanted to take out two teeth with one piece of string.
2   He had already done it before, with a different patient.
3   The 'dentist' lived in a very small house.
4   He had some very up-to-date equipment.
5   There were three patients in the waiting room when the real dentist arrived.

Word Puzzle

One word in each of the lines below is spelt wrongly. Put the letters in the correct order, and then write the word in the correct box. This will produce a word in the vertical box. Who does the word describe?

– The *stendit*. Is he good?
– I've got a *nipa* . . . in my mouth.
– And was the *tac* all right?
– I don't want the *hermam*!
– This is the first time I've taken out a *larom*.
– A pair of *scrossis*?

Communicating

1   Talking to Strangers

Listen to the first part of the sketch again. The man tries several times to start the conversation.

How would you start a conversation with someone, for example in a train compartment? Use the following expressions if they help. (Remember: If you start the conversation, you must have something to say when the stranger replies! e.g. You want a light or you want to open a window.)

Excuse me.	→ Yes?
I'm sorry to trouble you.	→ That's all right.

2   Making Excuses to Leave

Use these phrases to make apologies for leaving, adding a reason.

I'm sorry,	I can't stay. I have to go. I must be going.	I'm late for . . . .
I'm awfully sorry,	I must be on my way. I must be getting along.	I've got to . . . .

In Your Own Words

Re-enact the sketch in your own words, without reading from the text. Do it in short sections. These words will remind you:

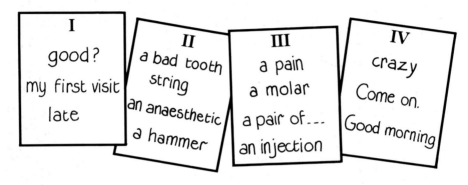

I
good?
my first visit
late

II
a bad tooth
string
an anaesthetic
a hammer

III
a pain
a molar
a pair of . . .
an injection

IV
crazy
Come on.
Good morning

Writing

A Letter to a Friend

The male patient in the sketch wrote a letter to a friend the following week. What do you think he wrote? Use the words below as a guide, and write his letter.

Dear Sheila,
    tell you/something/last week. pain/tooth/went/dentist. very nervous. lady/waiting-room/I arrived. I asked/dentist/good/didn't know. more nervous!
    The dentist arrived. wanted/take out/piece of string! knock out/hammer! completely mad. lady/I/managed/escape.
    leaving/passed/another dentist/stairs.
    Yours,
        Jack.
P.S. still/pain/tooth.

What Do You Think?

Nervousness

Which of the following makes you most nervous?
– a visit to the dentist
– flying
– high places
– horror films
– large crowds
Why?

7

Mr Williams and the Postman

SCENE   The front door of 65, Shakespeare Avenue
Early one morning

CHARACTERS   A postman
Mr Henry Williams [Mr W]
Mrs Agnes Williams [Mrs W]

I   *The postman walks up to the front door. He knocks at the door and rings the bell.*

POSTMAN   Good morning! Hello! Wake up!

                    Mr Williams opens the door.

                    Ah, good morning!

MR W   Good morning.

POSTMAN   Mr Williams?

MR W   Yes.

POSTMAN   Mr *H.* Williams?

MR W   That's right.

POSTMAN   Mr *Henry* Williams of 65, Shakespeare Avenue?

MR W   Sixty-five? Er . . . yes. Have you got anything for me?

POSTMAN   No.

MR W   No?

POSTMAN   No.

MR W	Then why did you wake me up?
POSTMAN	It's part of my job.
MR W	What? Waking people up?
POSTMAN	Yes. It's a new service from the Post Office.
MR W	Hmm. Listen – you're a postman.
POSTMAN	Yes.
MR W	And postmen bring letters.
POSTMAN	Yes.
MR W	But you haven't brought any for me.
POSTMAN	Wait a minute, Mr Williams. I'm sure I can find something for you. Um . . .

He takes three letters out of his bag.

Yes, here we are. Three letters. Which one would you like? The red one, the white one, or the blue one?

II　MR W	But those letters aren't for me.
POSTMAN	No, Mr Williams, but this is another new service from the Post Office – a new service for all those unhappy, unfortunate people who never get any letters.
MR W	Oh.
POSTMAN	And you, Mr Williams, you never get any letters, do you?
MR W	No, I don't.
POSTMAN	All right then, which one would you like? The red one, the white one, or the blue one?
MR W	Um . . . I'll have the red one, please.
POSTMAN	The red one is yours – if you can answer a simple question.
MR W	A question?
POSTMAN	Yes. Where does Queen Elizabeth the Second of England live?
MR W	Why? Have you got a letter for her?

He laughs.

POSTMAN	No, Mr Williams. That was the question. Where does Queen Elizabeth the Second of England live?
MR W	Where does Queen Elizabeth live?
POSTMAN	Yes.
MR W	I don't know.
POSTMAN	Mr Williams! It's easy! B-B-B-Buck –
MR W	Oh, yes! Buckingham Hotel.
POSTMAN	No, no! Palace!
MR W	Palace Hotel?
POSTMAN	No!
MR W	I know! Buckingham Palace!
POSTMAN	That's right! You've won the red envelope!
MR W	Oh, thank you! This is very exciting!

Mr Williams opens the red envelope.

There's nothing in it.

	POSTMAN	No, there's never anything in the red one.
III	MR W	This is ridiculous!
	POSTMAN	No, it isn't. There are still two more envelopes.
	MR W	Yes, but is there anything in them?
	POSTMAN	Of course there is.
	MR W	All right. The blue one.
	POSTMAN	Very well, Mr Williams. Here is the question for the blue envelope. What is the approximate population of Great Britain?
	MR W	Er . . . thirty-five million.
	POSTMAN	No. Higher.
	MR W	Eighty-five million?
	POSTMAN	No. Lower.
	MR W	Fifty-five million people!
	POSTMAN	– is the correct answer! You've won the white envelope!
	MR W	I don't want the white one. I want the *blue* one.
	POSTMAN	Oh, go on. Take the white one.
	MR W	I don't *want* the white one.
	POSTMAN	Oh, all right. Here's the blue one.
	MR W	Thank you.

Mr Williams opens the blue envelope.

		Hmm. Just a piece of paper.
	POSTMAN	What does it say?
	MR W	It says: 'You should have taken the white one.'
	POSTMAN	I told you.
	MR W	This is very silly. I'm going back to bed.
IV	POSTMAN	Wait a minute, Mr Williams. Today's *star prize* is in the white envelope.
	MR W	The star prize?
	POSTMAN	Yes.
	MR W	All right then, ask me the question.
	POSTMAN	Now listen carefully. If a man walks at five miles an hour, in the same direction as a car which is travelling at thirty miles an hour, how long will it take for the car to be 107 miles from the man?
	MR W	Eh?
	POSTMAN	Mr Williams! Concentrate! If a man walks at five miles an hour, in the same direction as a car which is travelling at thirty miles an hour, how long will it take for the car to be 107 miles from the man?
	MR W	I don't know. Three days?
	POSTMAN	No, no, Mr Williams. Look, why don't you ask your wife to help you?
	MR W	All right. Agnes!
	MRS W	Yes?
	MR W	Come here!
	MRS W	All right. I'm coming.

Mrs Williams comes to the door.

	POSTMAN	Ah, good morning, Mrs Williams.

MRS W	What's going on?
MR W	I'm trying to win the white one, Agnes.
MRS W	The white what?
MR W	The white envelope. I've already won the red one and the blue one.
MRS W	Henry, what *are* you talking about?
MR W	It's a competition. We answer questions and win prizes – and the star prize is in the white envelope.
POSTMAN	And here is the question for the white envelope. If a man walks at five miles an hour, in the same direction as a car which is travelling at thirty miles an hour, how long will it take for the car to be 107 miles from the man?
MRS W	That's easy. Four hours, sixteen minutes and forty-eight seconds.
POSTMAN	Four hours, sixteen minutes and forty-eight seconds is the correct answer! You have won today's star prize. Here you are.
MRS W	Ooh, thank you!
MR W	Well done, Agnes.
	Mrs Williams opens the white envelope.
	What is it?
MRS W	It's just a piece of paper.
POSTMAN	No, it isn't.
MR W	Yes, it is. Look! Just another piece of paper!
	They give the postman back the envelope and paper.
POSTMAN	But, Mr Williams . . . Mrs Williams . . .
MR W	Stop wasting our time. Come on, Agnes, let's go back to bed.
POSTMAN	But come back! I can explain!
	Mr and Mrs Williams go back into the house.
	I'm sure it's not just another piece of paper. There's always a prize in the white one. Let's have a look . . . It's a cheque . . . for £500! Mr Williams! Mrs Williams!
MR W	Go away!
POSTMAN	But Mr Williams, you've won the star prize!
MR W	Go away!!
POSTMAN	Oh. . . . Well, if Mr Williams doesn't want the £500, I think I'll keep it. . . . It's a lovely day today . . .
	He walks away, singing to himself.

V

Questions

I   1   What time of day was it?
     2   What was Mr Williams wearing?
II 3   What were the two new services from the Post Office?
     4   Which envelope did Mr Williams ask for first?
     5   Why was he annoyed when he got it?
III 6   Which envelope did he want next?
     7   When he answered the second question correctly, what did the postman offer him?
IV 8   Was the third question easier than the others?
     9   Why did Mr Williams call his wife?
   10 Did Mrs Williams answer the question quickly or slowly?
V 11 Why didn't Mr and Mrs Williams take the star prize?
   12 What was the star prize?

True or False?

These statements are all about the sketch. Are they *true* or *false*?

1   The postman gave Mr Williams three letters.
2   When Mr Williams asked for the red envelope, he knew that he had to answer a question.
3   The red envelope is always empty.
4   The star prize was in the white envelope.
5   Mr and Mrs Williams could not answer the third question.
6   Mr Williams was delighted with the star prize.

Word Puzzle

Fill in the words in the horizontal boxes. The letters in the vertical box will then spell a word: a quick way of sending letters.

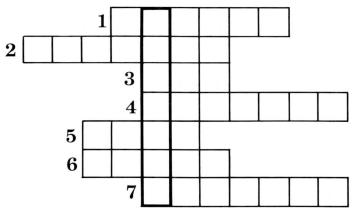

1   The Queen of England lives in one.
2   Waking people up is a new . . . . from the Post Office.
3   The colour of the first envelope.
4   The answer to the second question was: Fifty-five . . . . people.
5, 6 The . . . . was in the white envelope.
7   The postman didn't bring any for Mr Williams!

Communicating

Making Sure
A Listen to the first part of the sketch again. The postman is making sure of Mr Williams' exact name and address. Practise the six lines from 'Good morning.' to ' . . . 65, Shakespeare Avenue?'

Then practise similar dialogues in pairs. Use your own names and addresses, or give yourselves English names and addresses.

B Practise making sure of other facts and figures. First this dialogue at a railway station:

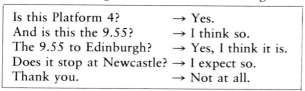

Is this Platform 4?	→ Yes.
And is this the 9.55?	→ I think so.
The 9.55 to Edinburgh?	→ Yes, I think it is.
Does it stop at Newcastle?	→ I expect so.
Thank you.	→ Not at all.

Then invent a similar dialogue in the queue at a cinema.

In Your Own Words
Re-enact the sketch in your own words, without reading from the text. Do it in short sections. These words will remind you:

I
Mr. Williams?
a new service
three letters

II
the red one
a question
nothing

III
the blue one
million
a piece of paper

IV
the star prize
the question
your wife
the correct answer

V
back to bed
a cheque

Writing

A Letter of Complaint
Mr Williams wanted to make a complaint about the postman. He wrote a letter to the Post Office.
Below is the part of the letter where Mr Williams explained what happened. The words are in the wrong order. Write the sentences correctly.

asleep was in bed I. heard ring woke I the door-bell when I up. the door to went I. your standing was of one postmen there. me didn't told he any for letters he have me. funny it was didn't I think.

Complete Mr Williams' letter, by writing the beginning and the end.

What Do You Think?

Prizes
Which of the following prizes would you like to win?
– A fortnight's holiday in Miami.
– A round-the-world cruise on a luxury liner.
– Free air travel for a year.
– The best stereo system in the world.
– A year's supply of food and drink.
– Dinner with your favourite film star or pop singer.
Give reasons for your choice.

8

The Bank

SCENE	The manager's office in a bank
CHARACTERS	Miss D. Posit, the bank manager
	Monica, Miss Posit's secretary
	Mr Moore, a customer
	A bank robber

I

Miss Posit is sitting at her desk. The intercom buzzes.

MISS POSIT   Yes, Monica?

MONICA   Miss Posit, there's a gentleman to see you. Mr Moore.

MISS POSIT   Ah, yes. Mr Moore. Bring him in please, Monica.

MONICA   Yes, Miss Posit.

Monica brings Mr Moore in.

Mr Moore.

MISS POSIT   Good morning, Mr Moore.

MR MOORE   Good morning.

MISS POSIT   Thank you, Monica.

Monica leaves the office.

Do sit down, Mr Moore.

MR MOORE   Thank you.

He sits down.

MISS POSIT   Now, Mr Moore, the situation is like this. Your account is in the red.

MR MOORE   Pardon?

MISS POSIT   In the red.

MR MOORE   I'm sorry. I don't understand.

MISS POSIT   In the red. Overdrawn.

MR MOORE   'Overdrawn'. No, I'm sorry. I've never heard that word before in my life.

MISS POSIT	It's very simple, Mr Moore. It means that you've taken more money *out* of the bank than you've put *in*.
MR MOORE	Oh, I see. Thank you very much.
MISS POSIT	I don't think you quite understand, Mr Moore. It means that you've put in *less* than you've taken out.
MR MOORE	Oh.
MISS POSIT	Your account is overdrawn. £200 overdrawn.
MR MOORE	£200 overdrawn. I see. Well, don't worry. I can put that right immediately.
MISS POSIT	Oh, good.
MR MOORE	Yes, I'll write you a cheque, shall I?
	He takes out his cheque-book and begins to write.
	Now . . . two hundred pounds . . .
MISS POSIT	Mr Moore, Mr Moore, if you write me a cheque for £200, you'll be overdrawn *more*, Mr Moore.
MR MOORE	I beg your pardon?
MISS POSIT	*More*, Mr Moore. M-O-R-E, *more*.
MR MOORE	No, no . . . *double-O* . . . M-double-O-R-E, Mr *Moore*. It *is* my name.
MISS POSIT	Mr Moore, I don't think you quite understand the situation. You see –
	The robber comes in suddenly.

II

ROBBER	Nobody move!
	Miss Posit continues speaking to Mr Moore.
MISS POSIT	– you see, if you write me a cheque for £200 –
ROBBER	I said: 'Nobody move!'
MISS POSIT	Can I help you?
ROBBER	That's better. *You* –
MR MOORE	Me?
ROBBER	Yes. Read this.
	He gives Mr Moore a note.
MR MOORE	Oh. O.K. (*Reading:*) 'Two pounds of tomatoes, six eggs, and a packet of chocolate biscuits.'
ROBBER	No, no, no. The other side.
MR MOORE	Oh, sorry. (*Reading:*) 'Give me all your . . . honey, or I'll . . . kiss you.'
ROBBER	Not *honey* – *money*.
MR MOORE	Oh, sorry. (*Reading:*) 'Give me all your *money*, or I'll kiss you.'
ROBBER	Not *kiss* – *kill*!
MR MOORE	Oh. Er . . . Miss Posit, I think this is for you.
	He gives the note to Miss Posit.
MISS POSIT	(*Reading:*) 'Give me all your money, or I'll kill you.' I see. Would you sit down for a moment?
ROBBER	Sit down?
MISS POSIT	Yes, I'm very busy at the moment. Please sit over there.
ROBBER	But –
MISS POSIT	I'll be with you in a moment.
	The robber sits down.

III	Now, Mr Moore. How much do you earn?
MR MOORE	£35 a week.
ROBBER	Excuse me –
MISS POSIT	Just one moment, *please*! . . . So you earn £35 a week. How much do you spend?
MR MOORE	£70 a week.
ROBBER	Excuse me –
MISS POSIT	One moment, *please*!! . . . £70 a week. So you spend twice as much as you earn.
MR MOORE	Yes, I earn half as much as I spend.
MISS POSIT	How do you do it?
MR MOORE	It's easy. I use my cheque-book.
MISS POSIT	Exactly, Mr Moore!
ROBBER	*Excuse me!*
MISS POSIT	Yes!!
ROBBER	*I* make £2,000 a week.
MISS POSIT	£2,000 a week? And how much do you spend?
ROBBER	£1,000 a week.
MISS POSIT	Really? So you *save* £1,000 a week.
ROBBER	Yes.
MISS POSIT	(*Very politely:*) Would you like to sit here?
ROBBER	Thank you.
MISS POSIT	Mr Moore, would you sit over there for a moment?
	The robber and Mr Moore change places.
	So you *save* £1,000 a week.
ROBBER	Yes.
MISS POSIT	Tell me . . . where do you keep this money?
ROBBER	Here. In this bag.
	He puts a large bag full of money on the desk.
MISS POSIT	Oh. Oh, yes. Very nice. Um . . . would you like to open an account, Mr . . . ?
ROBBER	Mr Steele.
MISS POSIT	Steele. I see. S-T-double-E-L-E?
ROBBER	Yes, that's right.
MISS POSIT	Well, just excuse me one moment, Mr Steele, and I'll get the necessary papers.
ROBBER	Certainly.
	Miss Posit leaves the office.
IV MR MOORE	Excuse me . . .
ROBBER	Yes?
MR MOORE	You make £2,000 a week.
ROBBER	Yes.
MR MOORE	How do you do it?
ROBBER	I rob banks.
MR MOORE	Oh, I see. You rob banks and *steal* the money.

ROBBER	Yes.
MR MOORE	How do you do it?
ROBBER	It's easy. You take a gun –
MR MOORE	I haven't got a gun.
ROBBER	Oh . . . well, borrow mine.
MR MOORE	Thank you very much.

Mr Moore takes the gun and fires it.

ROBBER	Be careful! . . . You take a gun and you take a note.
MR MOORE	Oh yes, the note. That's very good. I like that. (*Reading:*) 'Two pounds of tomatoes, six eggs –'
ROBBER	The other side!
MR MOORE	Oh, yes. (*Reading:*) 'Give me all your honey, or I'll kiss you!'
ROBBER	'*Money*' and '*kill*'!
MR MOORE	Oh, yes.
ROBBER	You take the note, go into the bank, and put the note on the bank manager's desk.
MR MOORE	Is that all?
ROBBER	Yes.
MR MOORE	I see.

V

Miss Posit comes back into the office.

MISS POSIT	Ah, yes. Now, Mr Steele –
MR MOORE	Give me all your honey . . . *money*, or I'll kiss . . . *kill* you.
MISS POSIT	Money, Mr Moore? Certainly. Take this bag.

She gives Mr Moore the robber's bag.

MR MOORE	Oh, thank you. That was easy.
ROBBER	Yes, but –
MISS POSIT	Mr Moore, your account is still £200 overdrawn.
MR MOORE	Oh, yes. Well . . . um . . . Here you are.

He gives her £200 from the robber's bag.

£50 . . . £100 . . . £150 . . . £200.

ROBBER	But . . . But . . .
MISS POSIT	Thank you, Mr Moore.
MR MOORE	Goodbye.

Mr Moore leaves.

MISS POSIT	Now, Mr Steele . . . your account . . .
ROBBER	But . . . But . . . But . . .
MISS POSIT	Mr Steele . . .
ROBBER	Just a minute! I think something's gone wrong. Hey, you! Come back! Bring back my money and my gun! Come back!

He runs after Mr Moore.

MISS POSIT	(*On the intercom:*) Monica, would you bring me some coffee, please? Some *strong black* coffee . . .

Questions

I 1 Mr Moore said 'I don't understand'. Was it true?
  2 What suggestion did Mr Moore make?
II 3 What was written on the robber's note?
  4 Was the manager frightened of the robber?
III 5 Did the robber and Mr Moore both have a problem with money?
  6 Why did the manager suddenly speak to the robber politely?
IV 7 What did the robber explain to Mr Moore?
  8 What did he give Mr Moore?
V 9 How did Mr Moore pay the manager?
  10 Who was happy and who was unhappy at the end?

A Letter and Some Instructions

Read these twelve sentences. Six are from a letter (from the bank manager to a customer) and six are from some instructions (from the robber to another robber, explaining how to rob a bank).

Decide which sentences come from the letter and which sentences come from the instructions. Then put them in the correct order.

1 You will also need a note.
2 Yours sincerely, D. Posit (Manager).
3 Go into the bank and put the note on the manager's desk.
4 The amount is £352.
5 How to rob a bank. First, you'll need a gun.
6 Dear Mr Bennett.
7 If not, the bank will refuse to renew your cheque-book.
8 The manager will read the note and give you some money.
9 You won't have to fire it, just point it at the manager.
10 I am writing to inform you that your account is overdrawn.
11 It should say: Give me all your money or I'll kill you.
12 I hope you will correct this situation as soon as possible.

Word Puzzle

Fill in the correct words.

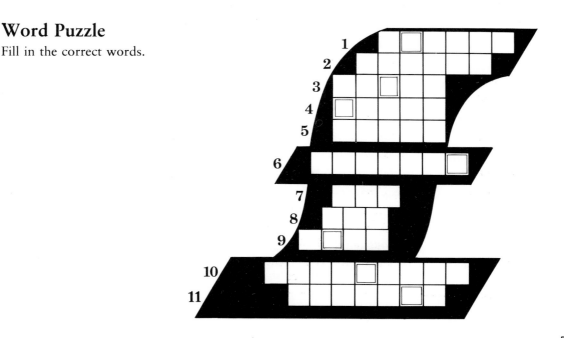

1 The bank . . . . had a gun and a note.
2 Mr Moore wanted to pay by . . . .
3 He wanted to . . . . a cheque for £200.
4 The robber's name sounded like the word '. . . . .'
5 Mr Moore . . . . twice as much as he earned.
6 His . . . . was not in the black.
7 The robber came to . . . . the bank.
8 Mr Moore's account was in the . . . .
9 Mr Steele did not really want to . . . . an account.
10 Mr Moore's account was £200 . . . .
11 The bank . . . . had a secretary called Monica.

When you have filled in all the words, take the letters in the special boxes. Arrange them into a word, one that is very similar to the manager's name.

Communicating

1 Paraphrasing
Listen again to the beginning of the sketch. Notice how the manager explained the situation to Mr Moore, particularly these lines:

> Miss Posit: Your account is *in the red*. . . .
> Mr Moore: I'm sorry. I don't understand.
> Miss Posit: In the red. Overdrawn. . . . It means that you've taken more money out of the bank than you've put in.

She first gave another word, and then explained.
Practise in pairs, making similar short dialogues. Start with these sentences:

1 This passport *has expired*.
2 This £5 note is *a forgery*.
3 This necklace is *priceless*.

2 Telling Someone How to do Something
Listen again to section IV of the sketch. Notice how the robber told Mr Moore how to rob a bank, using the Present Simple tense:

> Mr Moore: How do you do it?
> Robber: You take a gun . . . and you take a note. . . . You take the note, go into the bank, and put the note on the bank manager's desk.

In pairs, practise similar explanations. You can explain how to:

– make an omelette
– make a cup of tea
– send a telegram

or choose something else. Remember these phrases:

How do you do it?	First, you . . . .
What do you do first?	Then you . . . .
What do you do next/then?	After that, you . . . .
What do you do after that?	

In Your Own Words

Re-enact the sketch in your own words, without reading from the text. Do it in short sections. These words will remind you:

I
in the red
£ 200
a cheque

II
Read this.
honey
sit down

III
£ 35
£ 2,000
open an
account ?

IV
How___?
a gun
a note

V
Certainly
£ 200
Come back!

Writing

A List of Instructions

Choose one of the following, and write the necessary list of instructions:

(a) *A recipe.* Explain how to cook a dish. Choose one that you can do very well. Write first the *ingredients*, and then the method of making the dish (in a numbered list).
(b) *Making a telephone call.* Explain how to make a telephone call from a public telephone in your country. Write first the coins needed, and then the method of making the call (in a numbered list).

What Do You Think?

Pay

Mr Moore earned £35 a week, and the bank robber made £2,000 a week. Some people earn much more money than others. Do you think this is right? Who should earn a lot of money? Which would you prefer: a job you enjoyed, but which was badly paid? Or a job you hated, but which was well paid?

9
World Record

	SCENE	A TV studio
	CHARACTERS	Michael Moonshine
		Albert Hargreaves
		Mrs Hargreaves
		Mabel Phillips
		A man
		George and Hilda, TV viewers
I	GEORGE	Hilda, what's on television?
	HILDA	Er . . .
		She looks at a newspaper.
		. . . a programme called 'Your chance to break a world record'.
	GEORGE	What's that?
	HILDA	(*Reading:*) 'The fascinating programme in which people try to break world records.'
	GEORGE	Oh, let's have a look at it.
		He switches on the television. The programme has just begun.
II	MICHAEL M	Thank you, thank you, thank you. Yes, ladies and gentlemen, this is the programme that gives *you* the chance to break a world record. We have here in the studio tonight two people who are trying to break world records. Let's meet them and see what they're doing. Tell me, sir, what is your name?
	ALBERT	Albert Hargreaves.

MICHAEL M	Albert Hargreaves. Well, Albert, what are you doing?
ALBERT	I'm standing on one leg in a bucket of hot soup.
MICHAEL M	Ladies and gentlemen, he's standing on one leg in a bucket of hot soup!

The audience applaud.

Albert, how long have you been standing on one leg in that bucket of hot soup?

ALBERT	I've been standing here for six hours and fifty-eight minutes.
MICHAEL M	And what is the world record for standing on one leg in a bucket of hot soup?
ALBERT	The world record is seven hours and three minutes, Michael.
MICHAEL M	Seven hours and three minutes! And you've been standing there for *six* hours and fifty-*nine* minutes now. Well, Albert, you've only got *four* more minutes to go!

The audience applaud.

Albert, you've been standing on one leg in that bucket of hot soup for almost seven hours now.

ALBERT	That's right, Michael.
MICHAEL M	Tell me – is the soup still hot?
ALBERT	Yes. My wife's been coming in every half-hour with more hot soup. Here she comes now.

Mrs Hargreaves comes in.

MRS HAR	Here you are, Albert.

She pours some hot soup into the bucket.

ALBERT	Aaargh!
MICHAEL M	Well, I'm glad it's *your* leg in the soup, Albert, and not mine.

The audience laugh.

III   Now we have another contestant in the studio, a very charming young lady. Can you tell the viewers your name?

MABEL	Mabel Phillips.
MICHAEL M	Mabel Phillips. Well, Mabel, what are *you* doing?
MABEL	I'm leaning on this brush.
MICHAEL M	She's leaning on a brush, ladies and gentlemen!

The audience applaud.

Mabel, how long have you been leaning on that brush?

MABEL	I've been leaning on this brush for three hours and seventeen minutes.
MICHAEL M	She's been leaning on the brush for three hours and seventeen minutes. What is the world record for leaning on a brush, Mabel?
MABEL	Thirty-seven hours and fifty-six minutes.
MICHAEL M	Thirty-seven hours and fifty-six minutes! And you've been leaning on that brush for three hours and seventeen minutes. Well, Mabel, you've got . . . three, four, five, six – you've got a long way to go!

The audience laugh.

IV   Well, Albert has been standing on one leg in his bucket of hot soup for *seven* hours and *one* minute, so he's only got *two* more minutes to go! Poor Mabel's got a *long* way to go. . . . And here is another young man – and he hasn't got any trousers on.

The audience laugh.

Now, sir, what are *you* doing?

MAN	I'm looking for my trousers.
MICHAEL M	I can see that. And how *long* have you been looking for your trousers?
MAN	I've been looking for my trousers for five minutes.
MICHAEL M	And what's the world record?
MAN	Pardon?
MICHAEL M	What's the world record for looking for trousers?
MAN	I'm not trying to break a world record. I took my trousers off to have a bath, and when I got out of the bath, my trousers were gone.
MICHAEL M	I see. Get out of the way! We're on television!

The audience laugh.

V   Sorry about that, ladies and gentlemen. Now back to Albert Hargreaves. Albert, you've been standing in that bucket of hot soup for seven hours and *two* minutes. Only *one* more minute to go, and you will break the world record. And here comes Mrs Hargreaves with more hot soup!

MRS HAR	Here you are, Albert.

She pours some more soup into the bucket.

ALBERT	Aaaargh!
MICHAEL M	Tell me, Albert, how does it feel?
ALBERT	Hot!

The audience laugh.

MICHAEL M	No, no, no! How does it feel to be approaching the world record?
ALBERT	Well, Michael, I've been dreaming about this moment, I've been thinking about nothing else –
MICHAEL M	Yes, Albert.
ALBERT	– I've been practising every day –
MICHAEL M	Yes, Albert.
ALBERT	*Twice* on Sundays!
MICHAEL M	Yes – and here comes Mrs Hargreaves.
ALBERT	Oh no, not again!
MICHAEL M	It's all right, Albert, she's only looking at her watch!

The audience laugh.

MRS HAR	Albert! Albert! Only ten seconds to go! Ten, nine, eight, seven –

Mabel pushes Albert.

MABEL	(*Ironically:*) Congratulations, Albert!
ALBERT	Aaaargh!

Albert falls over.

HILDA	George, did you see that?
GEORGE	No. What happened?
HILDA	Mabel Phillips knocked him over with her brush!
MICHAEL M	Well, ladies and gentlemen, Albert Hargreaves *hasn't* broken a world record, but he *has* broken . . . his leg!!

The programme ends.

Questions

I 1 Had George and Hilda seen the TV programme before?
II 2 Do you think any of the people in the TV studio were well-known?
   3 What was Albert Hargreaves trying to do?
   4 Did Albert have a chance of being successful?
   5 How did he keep the soup hot?
III 6 What is the world record for leaning on a brush?
   7 Was Mabel Phillips close to breaking the record?
IV 8 Why did the 'young man' go on TV without his trousers?
V 9 Had Albert practised a lot?
   10 Why didn't he break the world record?

True or False?

On the day of the TV programme, the following 'preview' appeared in a newspaper. Was it an accurate 'preview'?

Your chance to break a world record (BBC TV, 8 p.m.)

The fascinating programme in which people try to break world records. Introduced by Michael Sunshine.

Tonight, Arnold Hargreaves will try to break the world record for standing in a bucket of hot water, and Muriel Phillips will try to hold a brush for longer than anyone else. She'll be there for quite a long time because the world record is more than two days! Arnold has been practising three times a week for his world record attempt.

Word Puzzle

Look at the boxes below. Choose one word from each box, making sure that it fits with the words before and after. The words will form a question and there is only *one* possible correct question.

If	is	moon	try	at	eat	trees
Why	do	dog	enjoy	of	break	clouds
Which	was	people	can	to	know	records

?

When you have found the question, answer it.

Communicating

Getting Information: Interviews

In the TV programme, Michael Moonshine interviewed people doing extraordinary things. He asked questions like:

> What is your name?
> What are you doing?
> How long have you been -ing . . .?
> What is the world record for -ing . . .?
> How does it feel to be -ing . . .?

In pairs, improvise dialogues between an interviewer and one of these people:

1 Someone sitting on top of a flagpole.
2 Someone walking from one end of the country to the other.
3 Someone trying to break the world record for eating eggs.
4 Someone preparing to walk across Niagara Falls on a tightrope.

In Your Own Words
Re-enact the sketch in your own words, without reading from the text. Do it in short sections. These words will remind you:

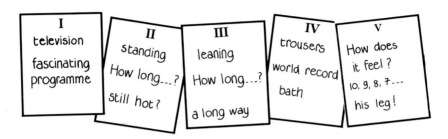

Writing

A Newspaper Article
Write a short newspaper article, describing the events in the 'World Record' TV programme. First make notes on these points:

– Albert Hargreaves – his world record attempt – his preparation – his wife.
– Mabel Phillips – her world record attempt – her feelings.
– The other man's interruption.
– What Mabel did to Albert.

Then use your notes to write the article. Give it a headline, for example: WORLD RECORD ATTEMPT FAILS.

What Do You Think?

The Olympic Games
Every four years, athletes try to break world records at the Olympic Games. Sometimes they only have ten seconds to prove they are the best in the world. The tension is terrible, and none of the athletes seem to be having a good time. Why do you think they do it? Are the Olympic Games a good thing?

The Superlative Vacuum~cleaner

SCENE	The hall of a house
CHARACTERS	A vacuum-cleaner salesman
	A housewife

I

The salesman rings the door-bell several times.

HOUSEWIFE	Yes, I'm coming.
	She opens the door.
	Good morning.
SALESMAN	Good morning, young lady. Is your mother in?
HOUSEWIFE	My mother? I'm the mother in this house. What do you want?
SALESMAN	Dust, madam.
HOUSEWIFE	Dust?
SALESMAN	Yes, madam. Dust.
HOUSEWIFE	I haven't got any dust.
SALESMAN	Oh yes you have!
	He shakes dust onto the floor from a paper bag.

		All over your carpet!
	HOUSEWIFE	Hey! I've just cleaned this carpet! Why are you putting dust all over it?
	SALESMAN	Don't worry, madam. I've got the answer to all your problems *here*! The Superlative vacuum-cleaner!
	HOUSEWIFE	The Superlative vacuum-cleaner? Why's it called 'Superlative'?
	SALESMAN	Because, madam, everything about it *is* superlative. It's the quickest, the cleanest, the cheapest, the smallest, the smartest, the most economical, the most effective, the most beautiful, the most revolutionary vacuum-cleaner in the world. And it's only £65.
II	HOUSEWIFE	Are you trying to sell me a vacuum-cleaner?
	SALESMAN	Yes, madam.
	HOUSEWIFE	Well, go on, then.
	SALESMAN	I've finished, madam.
	HOUSEWIFE	Finished? You haven't said very much. What sort of a vacuum-cleaner salesman are you?
	SALESMAN	Not a very good one, I'm afraid.
	HOUSEWIFE	I can see that.
	SALESMAN	No, I'm a very *bad* vacuum-cleaner salesman. In fact, I'm the worst salesman in our company.
	HOUSEWIFE	The worst?
	SALESMAN	The worst. I sometimes think I'm the worst vacuum-cleaner salesman in the world.
	HOUSEWIFE	Oh, dear. Do you . . . like your job?
	SALESMAN	Like my job? No, madam. I detest my job. It's the most boring job in the world. Every day it's the same: 'Good morning, young lady. Is your mother in? . . . The Superlative vacuum-cleaner . . . The quickest, the cleanest, the cheapest, the smallest . . .'
	HOUSEWIFE	Well, *is* it the quickest?
	SALESMAN	No, it's probably the slowest.
	HOUSEWIFE	Is it the cleanest?
	SALESMAN	Cleanest? Don't make me laugh! I don't think there's a dirtier vacuum-cleaner on the market. And it certainly isn't the cheapest either.
III	HOUSEWIFE	No, no, no. This is no good at all.
	SALESMAN	Pardon?
	HOUSEWIFE	Look, do you want to sell this vacuum-cleaner or don't you?
	SALESMAN	I suppose so.
	HOUSEWIFE	Well, your sales technique is all wrong.
	SALESMAN	Is it?
	HOUSEWIFE	Yes. I could sell vacuum-cleaners better than you.
	SALESMAN	No, you couldn't.
	HOUSEWIFE	Yes, I could. I'll show you. You come into the house, and I'll ring the bell and sell the vacuum-cleaner to you.
	SALESMAN	*You'll* sell the vacuum-cleaner to *me*?
	HOUSEWIFE	Yes.
	SALESMAN	O.K. But it isn't as easy as you think.
	HOUSEWIFE	We'll see. Go inside and shut the door.

SALESMAN		All right.
IV		*The salesman goes into the house and closes the door. The housewife rings the bell. The salesman opens the door.*
	SALESMAN	Not today, thank you.
		He closes the door. The housewife rings the bell again. The salesman opens the door again, and speaks in a high voice.
		Yes?
	HOUSEWIFE	Hello!
	SALESMAN	Hello.
	HOUSEWIFE	My goodness me, what a beautiful house you've got!
	SALESMAN	Ooh, do you like it?
	HOUSEWIFE	Like it? It's the most beautiful house I've seen for a long time.
	SALESMAN	Thank you very much.
	HOUSEWIFE	May I come in?
	SALESMAN	Er . . .
	HOUSEWIFE	Thank you. Oh, what a colourful carpet!
	SALESMAN	Yes, it's lovely, isn't it?
	HOUSEWIFE	It's the most colourful carpet I've seen for ages. I should think it was very expensive.
	SALESMAN	The most expensive one in the shop.
	HOUSEWIFE	And I suppose you've got a very good vacuum-cleaner to look after it.
	SALESMAN	A vacuum-cleaner? No, I haven't.
	HOUSEWIFE	You haven't got a vacuum-cleaner?
	SALESMAN	No.
	HOUSEWIFE	Well, madam, this is your lucky day, because I have *here* the best vacuum-cleaner that money can buy: the Superlative vacuum-cleaner.
	SALESMAN	Is it really good?
	HOUSEWIFE	Good? Good? It's the . . . the . . .
	SALESMAN	(*In his own voice:*) Quickest.
	HOUSEWIFE	. . . the quickest, the . . .
	SALESMAN	Cleanest.
	HOUSEWIFE	. . . the cleanest, the cheapest, the smallest, the smartest, the most economical, the most effective, the most beautiful, the most revolutionary vacuum-cleaner in the world.
	SALESMAN	(*In a high voice again:*) Ooh! How much is it?
	HOUSEWIFE	Just £65 to you, madam.
	SALESMAN	I'll buy one.
	HOUSEWIFE	Good.
	SALESMAN	(*In his own voice:*) Er . . . where's the money?
	HOUSEWIFE	It's in my handbag on the kitchen table.
	SALESMAN	Oh, right. (*In the high voice:*) I'll just go and get some money.
		He goes to the kitchen to get the money.
	HOUSEWIFE	Good idea, madam. You've made the right decision.
		The salesman comes back, speaking in his own voice.

SALESMAN	Do you know, you're a fantastic saleswoman.
HOUSEWIFE	Ooh!
SALESMAN	You've got a fantastic sales technique.
HOUSEWIFE	Do you think so?
SALESMAN	Yes, you've got the best sales technique I've seen all day.
HOUSEWIFE	Thank you!
SALESMAN	Thank *you*, madam.

He leaves and closes the door.

(*Speaking to himself, counting the money:*) Ten, twenty, thirty, forty, fifty, sixty, sixty-five. Now *that's* the way to sell a vacuum-cleaner.

Questions

I   1   Why did the salesman say: 'Is your mother in?'
      2   Why did he put dust on the carpet?
      3   Why was the vacuum-cleaner called the 'Superlative' vacuum-cleaner?
II   4   Did the housewife think he was a good salesman?
      5   Did the salesman think he was good?
      6   How did he describe his job?
III   7   What did the housewife think his problem was?
      8   What did she suggest?
IV   9   How did the housewife begin her 'sales talk'?
    10   Did the salesman sell the vacuum-cleaner?

What Happened Next?

Read these four possible continuations of the sketch. Choose the one which you think is most probable.

1 The housewife was delighted with her new vacuum-cleaner. She tried it immediately and it worked very well. She telephoned her husband at his office, to tell him that she had spent some of their holiday money.

2 The housewife went back into the kitchen. Suddenly she realized what she had done. She had bought a vacuum-cleaner that she didn't want, and she had spent £65 of her holiday money. 'Oh, well,' she said, 'at least I helped someone today.' She made herself a cup of tea.

3 The housewife realized what she had done immediately. She opened the door and ran down the garden path. The salesman was getting into his car. 'Just a minute,' said the housewife, 'I want my money back.' 'All right,' said the salesman, 'Here you are. £65.'

4 When the housewife realized what she had done, she opened the door and called to the salesman. 'I don't want this vacuum-cleaner,' she said. 'Give me my money back.' 'I'm sorry,' said the salesman. 'You've got the vacuum-cleaner, and I've got the money.' The housewife was furious: 'I'm going to call the police,' she said.

Word Puzzle

What are the opposites of the words below? (The answers were all used in the sketch.)

ugliest   1   _ _ _ _ / ☐ _ _ _ _ _ _ _ _
most expensive   2   _ _ _ ☐ _ _ _ _
most untidy   3   _ _ _ ☐ _ _ _ _
biggest   4   _ _ ☐ _ _ _ _ _
noisiest   5   _ _ ☐ _ _ _ _ _
dirtiest   6   _ _ _ _ ☐ _ _ _

Put the boxed letters in these boxes:

    1   2   3   4   5   6

   ☐   ☐   ☐   ☐   ☐   ☐

There is one letter missing. Here is a clue to it: In the sketch, the housewife asked: 'What sort of a vacuum-cleaner salesman are you?' Read the salesman's answer. The missing letter is the *first* letter of one of the words in his answer.

What does the word in the boxes mean?

Communicating

1 Complimenting

Listen to the first half of section IV of the sketch again. Notice how the housewife, as a saleswoman, says complimentary things about the house:

> What a beautiful house you've got!
> It's the most beautiful house I've seen for a long time.
> Oh, what a colourful carpet!

Practise in pairs, complimenting and accepting compliments about clothes. Use these expressions:

Your (dress) is really lovely.
It's a beautiful colour.
It really suits you.
It fits you perfectly.

Thank you.
Oh, do you like it?
It's very nice of you to say so.
Do you think so?

You can also practise complimenting someone on: their new car, a painting they have done, their garden.

2 Persuading Someone to Buy Something

If you want to sell something, you have to say how good it is. (Remember how the salesman described the vacuum-cleaner.) Practise selling things to one another. You can use anything: pens, books, watches, rings, etc. Practise in pairs. The 'salesman' can use some expressions from the first list; the 'customer' can use some expressions from the second list.

It's as good as new.
I've only had it for a few weeks.
It works perfectly.
I've hardly used it.
They're much more expensive these days.
I'll let you have it half price.

I don't really need one.
I'm not sure.
I'll think about it.
It looks like a bargain.
It's a bit expensive.
O.K. I'll take it.

In Your Own Words

Re-enact the sketch in your own words, without reading from the text. Do it in short sections. These words will remind you:

Writing

An Advertisement

Look at this advertisement for a car, and then write your own advertisement for the Superlative vacuum-cleaner.

What Do You Think?

Advertisements

We are surrounded by advertisements and people trying to sell us things. We see advertisements on TV, in the street and in the newspapers. Sometimes, people come to the door and try to sell us things.

Do we need so much advertising? Wouldn't it be better if we could choose what we wanted, without all the advertisements and salesmen?

11

Superman and the Psychiatrist

SCENE	A psychiatrist's consulting-room
CHARACTERS	A psychiatrist
	Angela, the psychiatrist's receptionist
	Mr Wilkins
	Superman

I   *The receptionist comes in.*

PSYCHIATRIST   Who's next, Angela?

RECEPTIONIST   There's a man to see you, doctor. His name is Wilkins. He says he can't talk quietly. He can only shout.

Mr Wilkins shouts from outside the door.

MR WILKINS   Can I come in?!!

PSYCHIATRIST   Hmm. Yes, I see. Ask him to come in.

RECEPTIONIST   Come in, Mr Wilkins.

MR WILKINS   Thank you!!

He comes in. The receptionist goes out.

Hello, doctor. Sorry to trouble you.

PSYCHIATRIST   That's all right, Mr Wilkins. Do sit down.

Mr Wilkins sits down.

II		Now . . . what seems to be the trouble?
	MR WILKINS	Well, doctor, I can't talk quietly. I can only shout.
	PSYCHIATRIST	(*Shouting:*) How long have you been like this?
	MR WILKINS	Pardon?
	PSYCHIATRIST	(*Back to normal:*) How long have you been like this?
	MR WILKINS	About a week.
	PSYCHIATRIST	Well, don't worry. I think you've got a very nice shouting voice.
	MR WILKINS	But I can't go on like this. I'll lose my job.
	PSYCHIATRIST	What *is* your job?
	MR WILKINS	I'm a librarian. I work in a library. I can't shout at work, you know.
	PSYCHIATRIST	In that case, Mr Wilkins, I think you should change your job.
	MR WILKINS	But what can I do? No-one wants a man who can only shout.
	PSYCHIATRIST	You could get a job as an English teacher.
	MR WILKINS	An English teacher?
	PSYCHIATRIST	Yes, they shout all the time.
	MR WILKINS	All right, doctor. I'll do that. Goodbye.
	PSYCHIATRIST	Goodbye, Mr Wilkins.
		He leaves, still shouting.
	MR WILKINS	Hey, you! Write down this verb!
	RECEPTIONIST	Goodbye, Mr Wilkins.
		The receptionist comes back into the room.
		Is Mr Wilkins all right, doctor?
	PSYCHIATRIST	Yes. He's going to be an English teacher.
	RECEPTIONIST	Oh.
III	PSYCHIATRIST	Who's next?
	RECEPTIONIST	Superman.
	PSYCHIATRIST	Superman?
	RECEPTIONIST	Yes.
	PSYCHIATRIST	Oh, I see . . . someone who *thinks* he's Superman.
	RECEPTIONIST	No, doctor. He really *is* Superman.
	PSYCHIATRIST	What? The big, strong man who flies through the air?
	RECEPTIONIST	Yes.
	PSYCHIATRIST	Oh, I see. Ask him to come in.
	RECEPTIONIST	Yes, doctor. (*To Superman:*) Come this way, please.
		Superman comes in, very tired and out-of-breath.
	SUPERMAN	Thank you.
	PSYCHIATRIST	Thank you, Angela.
		The receptionist goes out.
		Good morning, Mr . . . er . . .
	SUPERMAN	Superman.
	PSYCHIATRIST	Yes, Superman. Do sit down.
		Superman sits down.
	SUPERMAN	Thank you.

PSYCHIATRIST	Well, what seems to be the trouble?
SUPERMAN	Well, doctor, I'm Superman. People think I can do everything, but I can't. I can't do *anything* any more.
PSYCHIATRIST	What can't you do?
SUPERMAN	I can't climb buildings, I can't lift cars . . . and I can't fly.
PSYCHIATRIST	Well, don't worry. A lot of people have that problem.
SUPERMAN	But you don't understand. I'm Superman. If you can't fly, you can't be Superman. It's in the contract.
PSYCHIATRIST	Ah yes, I see.
SUPERMAN	In the old days, when people called for Superman, I could run into a telephone-box, take off my boring grey city suit, and become Superman, all in ten seconds. Yesterday, I went into a telephone-box, and it took me fifteen minutes just to take off my trousers. And when I came out, I couldn't remember where I was going. What do you think of that?

The psychiatrist is asleep.

Eh?

IV	PSYCHIATRIST	(*Waking up:*) What? Pardon?
	SUPERMAN	What do you think?
	PSYCHIATRIST	I think you should change your job.
	SUPERMAN	But what can I do?
	PSYCHIATRIST	Well, you've got a very nice face. You could be a pop singer.
	SUPERMAN	A pop singer?
	PSYCHIATRIST	Yes. Can you sing?
	SUPERMAN	No, I can't.
	PSYCHIATRIST	Can you dance?
	SUPERMAN	No.
	PSYCHIATRIST	Can you play the guitar?
	SUPERMAN	No.
	PSYCHIATRIST	So – you can't sing, you can't dance, and you can't play the guitar.
	SUPERMAN	That's right.
	PSYCHIATRIST	Well, you could be an *excellent* pop singer.
	SUPERMAN	What?
	PSYCHIATRIST	Yes, I can see it all now. Your name will be in lights! You'll be famous!
	SUPERMAN	But I *am* famous. I'm *Superman*.
	PSYCHIATRIST	Not any more. From today, you are Rocky Superdazzle!
	SUPERMAN	Do you think it's a good idea?
	PSYCHIATRIST	Yes, of course . . . Rocky.
V		*The receptionist comes in again.*
	RECEPTIONIST	Doctor –
	PSYCHIATRIST	Yes, Angela?
	RECEPTIONIST	– Mr Wilkins is back again.
		Mr Wilkins comes in, shouting as before.
	MR WILKINS	Yes, I am. I've changed my mind. I don't want to be an English teacher. What else can I do?
	PSYCHIATRIST	Don't worry, Mr Wilkins. I've got another job for you. You can work with Rocky Superdazzle here.
	SUPERMAN	How do you do?
	MR WILKINS	Rocky Superdazzle? That's not Rocky Superdazzle! That's Superman. I saw him in a telephone-box yesterday. Superman! Huh! It took him fifteen minutes just to take off his trousers.
	PSYCHIATRIST	Well, he *was* Superman, but he's not Superman any more. I think you can both work together . . .
		A few weeks later, at a pop concert.
	MR WILKINS	Ladies and gentlemen, you've heard of Rod Stewart! You've heard of Mick Jagger! You've heard of Queen Elizabeth the Second of England! Well, tonight we present a new star on the pop scene. He's *sexier* than Rod Stewart! He's *wilder* than Mick Jagger! And he's . . . *taller* than Queen Elizabeth the Second of England! Ladies and gentlemen – Rocky Super-dazzle!
		The audience screams and applauds.
	SUPERMAN	Thank you! Thank you very much! Thank you!

Questions

I   1   Was Mr Wilkins the psychiatrist's first patient that day?
II   2   Why was Mr Wilkins worried about his job?
      3   What job did the psychiatrist suggest for Mr Wilkins?
III   4   Why was Superman worried about his job?
      5   What happened to Superman the day before he saw the psychiatrist?
      6   Why did the psychiatrist fall asleep?
IV   7   Why did the psychiatrist tell Superman to become a pop singer?
      8   Name three things that Superman couldn't do.
V   9   Why did Mr Wilkins come back?
   10   Had Mr Wilkins met Superman before?

Read and Complete

Read these three possible continuations of the sketch, and put in the missing words.

1 Superman kept his (1) ...... name, and was a great success (2) ...... a pop singer. He and his (3) ....., the Supermen, had twenty hit records (4) ...... their first year. His voice was (5) ...... terrible, but he (6) ...... a fortune. People bought millions (7) ...... his records. He was most (8) ...... in America and Scotland.

2 Superman (9) ...... a record: 'What can I do?' by the Rocky Superdazzle Band. No-one bought it (10) ...... his mother. She only (11) ...... to it once, because his (12) ...... was absolutely terrible. Quite a (13) ...... of people came to his first concert, but (14) ...... twelve came to his second. No-one at (15) ...... came to his third. He (16) ...... a bank clerk.

3 Superman got a contract (17) ...... a record company. (The publicity manager (18) ...... the company liked his face). He took singing (19) ...... and improved his voice. At (20) ....., he wasn't very successful, and only sang (21) ...... small clubs. A year later, he (22) ...... on TV, and suddenly everyone wanted (23) ...... records. In fact, the records were very good.

Which continuation do you like best? Why?

Word Puzzle

All the answers in this puzzle begin with the letter 'S'.

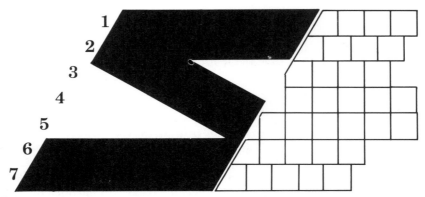

1 Mr Wilkins couldn't .... at work because he was a librarian.
2 When Mr Wilkins came into the psychiatrist's room, he said: '.......... to trouble you.'
3 The psychiatrist asked: 'What .... to be the trouble?'
4 The psychiatrist thought Mr Wilkins .... change his job.

5 The second patient wasn't . . . . who thought he was Superman – he *was* Superman.
6 Superman wasn't . . . . any more. He couldn't lift cars or climb buildings.
7 He became a pop . . . .

Communicating

1 Making Suggestions
In the sketch, the psychiatrist made some suggestions for jobs:

– to Mr Wilkins: You could get a job as an English teacher.
– to Superman: You could be a pop singer.

This form ('You could . . .') is an informal way of making suggestions. It is especially useful if you want to make several suggestions:

> You could . . . or you could . . . or you could always* . . .

* You add 'always' to your final suggestion if you don't think it is as good as the others.
Make suggestions to the people who have these problems:

1 There are no trains. How can I get to work?
2 I've won £1,000, and I don't know what to do with it.
3 Anna's phone is out of order. How can I contact her?
4 My neighbour always parks his lorry in front of my garage.

2 Predicting
Both Mr Wilkins and the psychiatrist spoke about the future:

> I can't go on like this. I'll lose my job.
> I can see it all now. Your name will be in lights! You'll be famous!

Continue these sentences with predictions:

1 Don't put boiling water in that glass. . . . .
2 I don't think you should give your grandfather a Rocky Superdazzle T-shirt for his birthday.
. . . .
3 Don't leave that box in front of the door. . . . .
4 You shouldn't work so hard. . . . .

In Your Own Words

Re-enact the sketch in your own words, without reading from the text. Do it in short sections.
These words will remind you:

71

Writing

A Newspaper Article

When Superman became a pop singer, a journalist interviewed him and wrote an article about him. These are the questions which the journalist asked Superman:

Why weren't you happy as 'Superman'?
Who gave you the idea of becoming a pop singer?
Can you sing/dance/play the guitar?
What kind of music do you play?
Have you made a record?

Write answers to the questions (in notes). Then write the newspaper article. It could begin like this:

SUPERMAN BECOMES POP SINGER
Superman is not Superman any more.
He is now Rocky Superdazzle. . . . .

Include some quotations from Superman.

What Do You Think?

Pop Singers

'Pop singers have a very easy life, and earn far too much money.' 'It's a hard life, being a pop singer.' What do you think? Would you like to be a pop singer?

12

The Travel Agency

SCENE	A travel agency in London
CHARACTERS	A travel agent
	Martin and Brenda Spencer

I

The travel agent is sitting at his desk in the travel agency. The phone rings.

TRAVEL AGENT   (*On the telephone:*) Honest Harry's Happy Holidays. Can I help you? . . . Oh, it's *you*, sir. . . . This is Perkins speaking, yes. . . . The holidays in Brighton? Well, I haven't sold very many . . . I'm doing my best, but people aren't interested in Brighton these days. . . . My job? Yes, I *do* like my job . . . Yes, I *do* want to *keep* my job. . . . Yes, sir. All right, I'll sell some holidays in Brighton. Yes, sir. Yes, sir. Goodbye.

He puts the phone down.

Oh, dear.

II

	Martin and Brenda come in.
MARTIN	Go on, Brenda.
BRENDA	Excuse me, is this a travel agency?
TRAVEL AGENT	No, madam. It's a fish and chip shop.
BRENDA	Oh, sorry. Come on, Martin.
TRAVEL AGENT	No, no, this *is* a travel agency. Just a little joke.
BRENDA	Oh.
TRAVEL AGENT	Yes, welcome to Honest Harry's Happy Holidays. Do sit down.
BRENDA	Thank you.
MARTIN	Thank you.
	They sit down.

III

TRAVEL AGENT	What can I do for you?
BRENDA	We'd like some information about holidays.
TRAVEL AGENT	Oh, good.
MARTIN	Yes, we'd like to go somewhere interesting.
TRAVEL AGENT	Somewhere interesting? Have you been to Brighton?
MARTIN	Brighton? No, we haven't –
TRAVEL AGENT	Really?
BRENDA	– and we don't want to, either.
TRAVEL AGENT	Why not?
MARTIN	Well, it's not *exciting*. We want to go somewhere *exciting*.
TRAVEL AGENT	I see. How about the Sahara Desert?
BRENDA	The Sahara Desert?
TRAVEL AGENT	Yes. Have you ever been there?
MARTIN	No, we haven't.
TRAVEL AGENT	Well, this is the holiday for you. Forty-five days in the middle of the Sahara Desert.
BRENDA	In the middle of the Sahara Desert? Is there anything to do?
TRAVEL AGENT	Oh yes, there's plenty to do. Have you ever been in a sandstorm?
MARTIN	A sandstorm? No, we haven't.
TRAVEL AGENT	Oh well, it's very exciting. There are sandstorms nearly every day. And lots of dangerous snakes. Have you ever been bitten by a dangerous snake?
MARTIN / BRENDA	No!
TRAVEL AGENT	Oh well, it's very exciting.
BRENDA	No, I don't think we'd like –
TRAVEL AGENT	Sandstorms, dangerous snakes, and, on the last day, a stampede of camels!
MARTIN	A stampede of camels? What's that?
TRAVEL AGENT	Haven't you ever seen a stampede of camels?
MARTIN	No.
TRAVEL AGENT	Oh, it's very exciting. You stand in the middle of three hundred camels, someone fires a gun in the air – Bang! – and all the camels get frightened and run away.
BRENDA	With us standing in the middle?

74

TRAVEL AGENT	Yes. Have you ever seen a frightened camel?
BRENDA	No. Is it exciting?
TRAVEL AGENT	Exciting? It's terrifying!
MARTIN	Isn't it dangerous?
TRAVEL AGENT	Of course it's dangerous! That's what makes it exciting!
MARTIN	Er . . . how much is it?
TRAVEL AGENT	£800.
BRENDA	£800!
TRAVEL AGENT	And £5 extra for the stampede of camels.
BRENDA	That's very expensive.
IV TRAVEL AGENT	Ah, I see. You want something cheaper. Um . . . how about the Arctic Ocean? Have you ever been to the Arctic?
MARTIN	No, we haven't.
TRAVEL AGENT	Well, we can give you three weeks in a small boat in the Arctic Ocean. Each boat has a small hole in the bottom –

BRENDA	A hole in the bottom?
TRAVEL AGENT	– and you have enough food for ten days.
MARTIN	Ten days?
TRAVEL AGENT	That's right.
MARTIN	But the holiday is for three weeks.
TRAVEL AGENT	That's what makes it exciting! And it's only £600.
BRENDA	£600! It's still much too expensive for us.
MARTIN	Have you got anything a little bit cheaper?
TRAVEL AGENT	Cheaper . . . well, I don't know. Let me see . . . Oh, yes. Now *this* is a holiday to remember. The Amazon jungle. Have you been to the Amazon jungle?
MARTIN	No, we haven't.
TRAVEL AGENT	Well, this may be the holiday for you. We drop you into the middle of the Amazon jungle by parachute –
MARTIN	By parachute!

TRAVEL AGENT	Yes, we drop you into the middle of the Amazon jungle, with a map –
BRENDA	Well, at least you get a map.
TRAVEL AGENT	– with a map of the London Underground.
BRENDA	Oh. I don't think we'd like that. It sounds very dangerous.
TRAVEL AGENT	Yes, but it's very *exciting*! This is the twentieth century. People want exciting holidays. *You* said *you* wanted an exciting holiday.
MARTIN	But all your holidays are dangerous, expensive, and too far away from home.
TRAVEL AGENT	Oh, I see. Now you want something nearer home.
MARTIN	Er . . . yes.

V

TRAVEL AGENT	Have you ever been to Spain?
MARTIN	No, we haven't.
TRAVEL AGENT	We can offer you a month, fighting the strongest bulls in Spain.
BRENDA	Bull-fighting? No, I don't want to do that.
TRAVEL AGENT	Oh. Have you ever been to Paris?
MARTIN	No, we haven't.
TRAVEL AGENT	What about ten days in Paris? . . .
MARTIN	That sounds marvellous!
TRAVEL AGENT	. . . painting the outside of the Eiffel Tower.
BRENDA } MARTIN }	No, thanks!
TRAVEL AGENT	Well, what about two weeks in Brighton?
BRENDA	No, thanks!
MARTIN	Just a minute. Did you say 'Brighton'?
TRAVEL AGENT	Yes. How about two weeks in Brighton, staying in a nice quiet hotel by the sea?
BRENDA	Well, yes . . .
MARTIN	Yes, that sounds wonderful!
TRAVEL AGENT	It's not very exciting. No camels, no snakes, but you can't have everything, can you?
BRENDA	No. That's very nice. We'll take it.
MARTIN	How much is it?
TRAVEL AGENT	£50 each, please. Could you just sign this form for the reservations?

He gives Martin a form.

Just here, please.

Martin signs.

Thank you. And here. And here. And here. And . . . here. Thank you.

BRENDA	Thank you very much.
MARTIN	Goodbye.
TRAVEL AGENT	Goodbye, and I hope you enjoy your holiday.

Martin and Brenda leave. The telephone rings.

(*On the telephone:*) Honest Harry's Happy Holidays. Can I help you? . . . Well, we've got some very nice holidays in Brighton, as a matter of fact . . .

Questions

I   1   Why was the travel agent worried about his job?
II   2   Why did he say: 'It's a fish and chip shop'?
III   3   Why didn't Martin and Brenda want to go to Brighton?
     4   Describe the holiday in the Sahara Desert.
     5   How much did that holiday cost?
IV   6   Describe the holiday in the Arctic Ocean.
     7   Why wasn't the map useful?
     8   Martin said something was wrong with all the holidays. What?
V   9   Describe the holidays in Spain and France.
   10   How much did Martin and Brenda pay for their holiday?

Read and Complete

Read this extract from the 'Honest Harry's Happy Holidays' brochure, and put in the missing words.

HOLIDAY NO. 247: THE SAHARA DESERT
45 days
£800 (£805 with stampede of camels)

Have you (1) . . . . . . visited the Sahara Desert? If not, this is the (2) . . . . . . for you. We can (3) . . . . . . you forty-five exciting days in the (4) . . . . . . of the Sahara Desert. You won't be bored (5) . . . . . . a moment, because there's always (6) . . . . . . to do. If you've (7) . . . . . . been in a sandstorm, don't miss this chance! There are (8) . . . . . . nearly every day. When you get home, you can (9) . . . . . . your friends all about the sandstorms you've (10) . . . . . . in – *and* about the (11) . . . . . . snakes you've seen. Holiday No. 247 is for (12) . . . . . . who want exciting holidays. If you are (13) . . . . . . of these people, this holiday is (14) . . . . . . you. It's certainly a holiday (15) . . . . . . remember!

Word Puzzle

Put the right words in the boxes.

         9   5   11   5   2   1

The Sahara is a ☐ ☐ ☐ ☐ ☐ ☐

       11   1   3   13   –   5   9   5

The ☐ ☐ ☐ ☐ ☐ ☐ ☐ ☐ of camels cost £5 extra.

                        7   2   14   –   12   1   8   10

Martin and Brenda finally chose a holiday in ☐ ☐ ☐ ☐ ☐ ☐ ☐ ☐

Now fill these boxes with the right letters:

1   2   3   4   5   6   7   2   8   3   9   5   10   11   1   12   5   13   14   10   9
☐ ☐ ☐ ☐ ☐ ☐   ☐ ☐ ☐ ☐ ☐ ☐ ☐ ☐   ☐ ☐ ☐   ☐ ☐ ☐ ☐

There are two letters missing. Can you guess them? Can you say what the expression means?

Communicating

1 Making Suggestions

In the sketch, the travel agent made several suggestions about holidays:

> How about the Sahara Desert?
> How about the Arctic Ocean?
> What about ten days in Paris?
> What about two weeks in Brighton?

In pairs, practice asking for suggestions and making suggestions about birthday presents, for example:

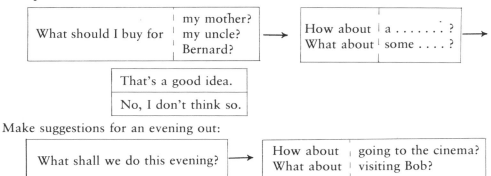

| What should I buy for | my mother? my uncle? Bernard? | → | How about What about | a . . . . ? some . . . . ? | → |

| That's a good idea. |
| No, I don't think so. |

Make suggestions for an evening out:

| What shall we do this evening? | → | How about What about | going to the cinema? visiting Bob? |

2 Polite Requests for Information

In the sketch, Brenda said 'We'd like some information about holidays'.
Practise asking for information about these things:

> holidays in Scotland/stereo equipment/central heating

Make dialogues like this:

> – Good morning. I wonder if you can help me. I'd like some information about . . . .
> – Certainly, sir/madam. What sort of . . . . . . are you interested in?
> – Well, something that's not too expensive.
> – I see.

In Your Own Words

Re-enact the sketch in your own words, without reading from the text. Do it in short sections.
These words will remind you:

I	II	III	IV	V
speaking	a travel	holidays	the Arctic Ocean	Spain
Brighton	agency	Brighton	the Amazon	Paris
my job	Welcome to...	the Sahara Desert	Jungle	Brighton
		expensive	expensive	Goodbye

Writing

An Extract from a Brochure
Look at the extract from the brochure ('Read and Complete', p. 77). Choose one of the other holidays:

– the Arctic Ocean
– the Amazon Jungle
– Spain
– Paris
– Brighton

and write a similar advertisement for it.

What Do You Think?

Travel
A   What is the worst holiday you've ever had? What is the best holiday you've ever had? Why was the bad one bad and the good one good?
B   If you had one year, and all the money you needed, what would be your perfect holiday? Plan a trip, starting in your town and lasting for one year.

13

Gerry Brown's Driving Test

SCENE	A car
CHARACTERS	Gerry Brown
	Brian Smith, Gerry's friend
	A driving examiner

I *Brian has just arrived at the test centre in his car. He is sitting in it, waiting for Gerry.*

BRIAN Hmm. . . . Three o'clock. Where is he? . . . Ah, there he is. Gerry! Gerry!

Gerry comes to the car.

	GERRY	Ah, hello!
	BRIAN	Hello, Gerry.
		Brian gets out of the car.
		Well, the big day, eh?
	GERRY	Yes, my driving test. It's very good of you to lend me your car.
	BRIAN	Oh, that's all right, Gerry. You *have* had driving lessons, haven't you?
	GERRY	Oh, yes. Well . . . I had *one.*
	BRIAN	One?
	GERRY	Yes. I had one last night. It was very good.
	BRIAN	One last night! That's not enough. You should have had at least *ten!*
	GERRY	Now don't worry. I've flown aeroplanes, you know, and it's all more or less the same. You just jump in, switch on, and up she goes!
	BRIAN	Yes, but this isn't an *aeroplane.* It's a *car. My* car!
	GERRY	Oh yes, I can see that.
II	BRIAN	Hmm . . . *that's* another problem.
	GERRY	What?
	BRIAN	Your eyes.
	GERRY	What's the matter with my eyes?
	BRIAN	Well, they're not exactly perfect, are they?
	GERRY	Well, I know I can't see very well, but –
	BRIAN	But you told the authorities that your eyes were perfect. You shouldn't have done that.
	GERRY	Yes, I know. But don't worry, everything will be all right. I borrowed these glasses from my uncle, and he says they're marvellous.
	BRIAN	Your *uncle's* glasses! But Gerry, you should have brought your *own* glasses.
	GERRY	I haven't got any of my own. But don't worry, my uncle has worn these for twenty-five years, and he's a brain surgeon.
	BRIAN	Gerry –
	GERRY	Look, I'll put them on.
		He puts on the glasses.
		There. Oh. . . . Um . . . Brian? . . . Brian?
		He bumps into the car.
		Oh!
III	BRIAN	Gerry, look, here comes the examiner.
	GERRY	Oh yes, I see. He looks like a very nice man.
	BRIAN	Gerry, it's not a *man.* It's a *woman.*
	GERRY	Oh.
	BRIAN	Now listen, Gerry. There's only one way you can pass this test.
	GERRY	Yes?
	BRIAN	Be polite.
	GERRY	Be polite?
	BRIAN	Yes. Be *very very* polite . . . and remember: Always open the door for a lady.

GERRY	Be polite, and open the door for a lady. Be polite and —
BRIAN	Shh, Gerry. Here she is.
	The examiner arrives.
EXAMINER	Mr Brown?
GERRY	Er . . . yes.
EXAMINER	I'm the examiner. Shall we get in?
GERRY	Er . . . yes. Allow me to open the door for you.
	He opens the door and the examiner gets into the car.
EXAMINER	Thank you.
	He closes the door.
GERRY	Was that all right?
BRIAN	Very good, Gerry. But I think I'll come with you, just in case.
GERRY	All right.
	Gerry and Brian get into the car. Brian sits in the back.

IV

EXAMINER	Now, Mr Brown. I'd like you to drive the car straight down the road.
GERRY	Straight down the road, yes.
	He tries to drive away. The car stalls.
	Oh. Sorry.
	He tries again, and drives away very fast.
EXAMINER	Turn right, Mr Brown.
	Gerry turns left.
BRIAN	Gerry! You turned *left*. She said 'Right'. You should have turned *right*.
GERRY	(*Cheerfully:*) Sorry.
EXAMINER	Turn left, Mr Brown.
	Gerry turns right.
BRIAN	Gerry! You turned *right*. You should have turned *left*.
EXAMINER	The traffic lights are red, Mr Brown.
BRIAN ⎫ EXAMINER ⎭	Red!
	Gerry stops the car at the traffic lights.
GERRY	Ha, ha! Very good, eh? Straight on?
EXAMINER	Er . . . n-n-no, Mr Brown. I think I'll get out here.
GERRY	Oh. Allow me to open the door for you.
EXAMINER	No, no, thank you. That won't be necessary.
	She gets out of the car and walks away.
	I should have stayed in bed today. I knew it . . . I knew it was going to be a bad day.
GERRY	Oh, dear.
BRIAN	I told you you should have had more lessons, Gerry.
GERRY	Ah, green!
	Gerry drives away very fast.
BRIAN	Gerry! Gerry! Slow down, Gerry! Gerry!!

Questions

I   1 Was Gerry confident about his driving test?
   2 Why was Brian nervous about Gerry's driving?
II 3 Had Gerry lied to anyone?
   4 Were the glasses useful to Gerry?
III 5 What advice did Brian give Gerry?
   6 Did Gerry follow his advice?
   7 Why did Brian get into the car, too?
IV 8 How many mistakes did Gerry make?
   9 Who was the calmest person in the car?
   10 Why did the examiner get out of the car?

Read and Complete

The text below is taken from the British 'Highway Code'. Read it and put in the missing words.

> Keep your vehicle (1) . . . . . good condition. Pay particular attention (2) . . . . . lights, brakes and tyres.
> Do not (3) . . . . . a journey if you (4) . . . . . tired. Never drive (5) . . . . . drinking alcohol.
> Do (6) . . . . . drive if you (7) . . . . . unwell.
> If you (8) . . . . . spectacles, wear them.
> Use your (9) . . . . . often, so that you can see what is behind you.
> Driving (10) . . . . . long distances may make you feel (11) . . . . . Make sure there is plenty of fresh (12) . . . . . in your vehicle. If you become tired (13) . . . . . a journey, stop and rest at a suitable parking place. You (14) . . . . . obey the speed limits for the road and (15) . . . . . your vehicle. Any speed limit is a maximum. It does (16) . . . . . mean that it is safe to (17) . . . . . at that speed.
> Go much more (18) . . . . . if the road is wet (19) . . . . . icy, or if (20) . . . . . is fog.

Word Puzzle

Put the correct words in the horizontal lines.

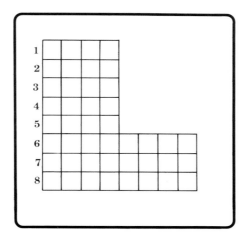

1 Gerry should . . . . . had more than one lesson.
2 Gerry's . . . . . weren't exactly perfect.

3 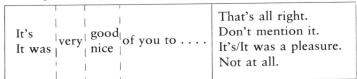 This sign means: Turn . . . . .

4 Gerry did not . . . . . his test.
5 When Gerry drove too fast, Brian told him to slow . . . . .
6 Gerry had two . . . . . : he couldn't drive properly, and his eyesight was bad.
7 The glasses weren't Gerry's. He had . . . . . them from his uncle.
8 Gerry was very polite to the . . . . ., but it didn't do any good.

When you have filled in all the words, look at the first letters of Nos. 1–4. They should spell a word, one which Brian might have shouted at the end of the sketch.

Communicating

1 Thanking Someone for a Favour
Look at these lines from the sketch:

Gerry	:	It's very good of you to lend me your car.
Brian	:	Oh, that's all right, Gerry.

Think of your own examples, and practice in pairs:

It's It was	very	good nice	of you to	That's all right. Don't mention it. It's/It was a pleasure. Not at all.

2 Giving Advice
In the sketch, Brian gave Gerry some advice. He said: 'There's only one way you can pass this test. . . . Be very very polite. . . . and always open the door for a lady.'
In pairs, make short dialogues. In each pair, Student A says what his/her problem is, and asks for advice. Here are some problems:

– My sister is very very angry.
– I've got hiccups.
– I've had a terrible cough for months.

Student B gives some advice, using the expression:

'There's only one way you can (calm her down). . . . .
(get rid of them). . . . . . .
(get rid of that cough) . . . .'

In Your Own Words

Re-enact the sketch in your own words, without reading from the text. Do it in short sections. These words will remind you:

Writing

Notes for a Report
These are the examiner's notes about Gerry's test:

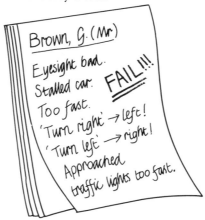

Use the notes to write the examiner's report on the test.

What Do You Think?

Tests and Examinations
Some people love tests and examinations. Most people don't like them very much. Do you dislike them? Why? What tests and examinations have you taken? Are tests and examinations necessary?

14

Giovanni's Café

SCENE	A pavement café in Rome
CHARACTERS	Geoffrey Burton
	Dorothy Burton, his wife
	Teresa Pilkington
	Giovanni

I

Geoffrey and Dorothy are sitting at a table in the café.

GEOFFREY	Well, here we are in Rome. The sun is shining, and we haven't got a care in the world.
DOROTHY	Yes, Rome is *so* beautiful.
GEOFFREY	And it's such a beautiful day.
DOROTHY	This square looks lovely in the sunshine.
GEOFFREY	And it's so nice, sitting here with you. No trains to catch . . .
DOROTHY	No telephones to answer . . .
GEOFFREY	No boring business people to talk to . . . Do you know, this is the first holiday we've had for five years – since we were married.
DOROTHY	And it's our first visit to Rome, too. It's like a second honeymoon.
GEOFFREY	Yes, and now we're alone together, with all the time in the world.
DOROTHY	Yes.

	GEOFFREY	Just you, and me, and romantic Rome.
	DOROTHY	Yes.
II		*Teresa comes to their table.*
	TERESA	Excuse me, do you speak English?
	GEOFFREY	Yes.
	TERESA	May I sit here?
	GEOFFREY	Er . . . oh . . . yes.
		Teresa sits down.
	TERESA	Thank you. Just a minute – it's Geoffrey – Geoffrey Burton!
	GEOFFREY	Good God! Teresa Pilkington!
	TERESA	Geoffrey, darling! How lovely to see you! It's been so long since we –
	GEOFFREY	Er . . . Teresa, this is my *wife*, Dorothy.
	TERESA	Oh, your wife. Delighted to meet you.
	DOROTHY	So you know Geoffrey, do you?
	TERESA	Oh yes, Geoffrey and I are old friends, aren't we, Geoffrey?
	GEOFFREY	No. Er . . . yes. Er . . . what are you doing in Rome, Teresa?
	DOROTHY	You're old friends, are you?
	TERESA	Oh yes, I've known Geoffrey for years and years, since we were both young and innocent.
	GEOFFREY	Goodness me! Look at that remarkable statue!
	DOROTHY	Geoffrey! . . . Tell me, Miss Pilkington, what exactly do you mean by 'young and innocent'?
	TERESA	Well, darling, before Geoffrey met me, he was just an innocent boy.
	GEOFFREY	Er . . . yes . . . we met at kindergarten.
	TERESA	Geoffrey, you know that's not what I mean.
	DOROTHY	Well, what exactly *do* you mean?
	GEOFFREY	Good Lord! Look at that magnificent telephone-box!
	DOROTHY	Geoffrey!
	GEOFFREY	Well, you don't see telephone-boxes like that in England, do you?
III	TERESA	Poor Geoffrey! Before he met me, his life was so boring. He was a student at an awful college in the mountains, and he hated every minute of it.
	DOROTHY	But Geoffrey – you told me you *loved* that college in the mountains!
	TERESA	Ah yes, that's because he met *me* there.
	DOROTHY	What – at the college?
	TERESA	No, in the mountains.
	GEOFFREY	Er, Dorothy, I think we'd better go. The Colosseum closes at six o'clock, you know.
	DOROTHY	Sit down, Geoffrey. It's only half past eleven.
	TERESA	Yes, I remember that day so well – the day that we met. The mountains were so beautiful, the sky was so blue –
	DOROTHY	– and Geoffrey was so *green*, I suppose.
	TERESA	'Green'? What do you mean?
	DOROTHY	'Green'. Young and innocent. Just the way you like them, I suppose.
	TERESA	Well, really!

Teresa gets up.

Excuse me! . . . Goodbye, Geoffrey. (*Sarcastically:*) Delighted to have met you, Mrs Burton.

GEOFFREY   Teresa . . . um . . .

TERESA   Goodbye, Geoffrey.

Teresa leaves.

IV GEOFFREY   Oh, dear.

DOROTHY   So before you met her, you were just an innocent boy! You told me I was the first woman in your life, and I believed you . . . and *I've* been *so* honest with *you*.

GEOFFREY   Yes, Dorothy.

DOROTHY   I've told you everything.

GEOFFREY   Yes, Dorothy, I know. I was the first man in your life.

DOROTHY   The first and *only* man, ~~Geoffrey~~. *Robbin*

Giovanni comes to the table.

GEOFFREY   Oh . . . waiter. I'll have a Martini, please.

GIOVANNI   Certainly, sir. And for you, madam? Oh! Dorothy!

DOROTHY   ~~Giovann~~i! *George*

GIOVANNI   Dorothy!

GEOFFREY   ~~Giovann~~i? *George*

GIOVANNI   Dorothy, it's wonderful to see you again!

GEOFFREY   Dorothy, have you met this man before?

DOROTHY   Well, ~~Geoffrey~~ – *Robbin*

GIOVANNI   Dorothy, it must be five years!

DOROTHY   Six, ~~Giovanni~~, six! *George*

GIOVANNI   And now you've come back to ~~Rome~~! *Bath*

GEOFFREY   Come back? What's he talking about?

DOROTHY   Well, ~~Geoffrey~~ *Robbin*

GIOVANNI   Come with me, Dorothy. We've got *so* much to talk about!

DOROTHY   Oh . . . er, yes . . . um . . . excuse me, ~~Geoffrey~~. *Robbin*

Giovanni and Dorothy leave.

GEOFFREY   Dorothy! Dorothy! Dorothy!

Questions

I
  1 Where were Geoffrey and Dorothy sitting?
  2 Had they been to Rome before?

II
  3 Did Dorothy know Teresa?
  4 Did Dorothy like Teresa?
  5 Why did Geoffrey say 'Look at that remarkable statue!'?

III
  6 Where did Geoffrey first meet Teresa?
  7 Why did Teresa get up and leave?

IV
  8 Dorothy said: 'I've told you everything.' Was this true?
  9 Was Dorothy surprised to see Giovanni?
  10 How did Geoffrey feel at the end?

Read and Complete

This is a postcard which Geoffrey and Dorothy sent from Rome to a friend in London. (They posted it before they met Teresa and Giovanni.) Read it and put in the missing words.

Dear Sandra,   August 17th

Here we are in Rome. We've been here ① .... three days, and we've ② .... very lucky with the weather. The sun's been ③ .... non-stop, and all the squares and fountains ④ .... very beautiful in the sunshine. It's so ⑤ .... , being away from London, with no trains to ⑥ .... and no ⑦ .... to answer. The city is full ⑧ .... tourists - perhaps we'll meet ⑨ .... we know!

Wish you were with us - Rome is ⑩ .... a beautiful city!

Dorothy & Geoffrey

Word Puzzle

All the answers in the puzzle on the next page are adjectives. They were all used in the sketch. When you have filled in all the words, the letters in the vertical box should all be the same.

1 This described Rome and the weather.
2 This described the statue.
3 This described the telephone-box.
4 This described the sky.
5 This described Geoffrey.

6 No. 5 meant 'young and . . . .'
7 'How . . . . to see you!'
8 '. . . . . to meet you.'
9 'It's . . . . to see you again.'
10 Dorothy said she had been . . . . with Geoffrey.

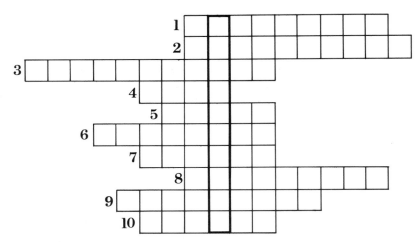

Communicating

1 Asking for Clarification

In the sketch, Dorothy asked Teresa: 'What exactly do you mean by "young and innocent"?'

Later, Teresa asked Dorothy: '"Green"? What do you mean?'

Use these ideas to practice asking for clarification:

Smoking is *bad for you*. Hard work is *a good thing*. Watching TV is *a waste of time*.	What exactly do you mean by '. . .'?
	'. . .' What do you mean?

2 Leaving Someone You've Just Met

When Teresa left, she said: 'Delighted to have met you.' This is a formal expression. You can also use these less formal expressions:

(It was) (very)	nice meeting you. nice to meet you.

In threes, practise like this:

A introduces B and C, and leaves them.
B and C ask each other about their jobs.
B then leaves C (e.g. to speak to someone else).

In Your Own Words

Re-enact the sketch in your own words, without reading from the text. Do it in short sections. These words will remind you:

Writing

A Postcard
Look at the postcard which Dorothy and Geoffrey wrote from Rome (p. 89). Imagine you are on holiday (choose a place), and write a similar postcard to a friend.
Say how long you've been there, what the weather is like, what you've seen, and how long you're going to stay. Add any other ideas you like.

What Do You Think?

Tourists
In the holiday season, tourists are everywhere: there are crowds of them on beautiful beaches, in pleasant little villages, on mountainsides, in city streets. Do tourists *spoil* these places? If your town council decided to ban tourists, what would you say?
Is it better to be a tourist in a large group, or a 'solo traveller'?

15
Shakespeare's House

SCENE	The living-room of a house in the town where Shakespeare was born
CHARACTERS	Sidney and Ethel, tourists
	A man

I — *Sidney and Ethel come into the room.*

SIDNEY — Well, Ethel, here we are in Shakespeare's front room. This must be where he wrote all his famous tragedies.

ETHEL	I'm not surprised, with furniture like this.
SIDNEY	What do you mean?
ETHEL	Well, look at that armchair. He can't have been comfortable, sitting there.
SIDNEY	Don't be silly! He probably sat at this table when he was writing tragedies.
ETHEL	Oh, yes . . . Look!

She shows Sidney a typewriter.

This must be Shakespeare's typewriter.

SIDNEY	Shakespeare's typewriter?
ETHEL	Yes. He must have written all his plays on this.
SIDNEY	Ethel! That can't be Shakespeare's typewriter.
ETHEL	Why not?
SIDNEY	Because Shakespeare didn't *use* a typewriter.
ETHEL	Didn't he?
SIDNEY	No, of course he didn't. He was a very busy man. He didn't have time to sit in front of a typewriter all day. He probably used a tape-recorder.
ETHEL	A tape-recorder?
SIDNEY	Yes. I can see him now. He must have sat on this chair, holding his microphone in his hand, saying: 'To be, or not to be.'
ETHEL	What does that mean?
SIDNEY	Ah well, that is the question.

II	ETHEL	Sidney, look!
	SIDNEY	What?
	ETHEL	Over here. This must be Shakespeare's television.
	SIDNEY	Shakespeare's television?
	ETHEL	Yes, it must be. It looks quite old.
	SIDNEY	Shakespeare didn't have a *television*.
	ETHEL	Why not?
	SIDNEY	Why not? Because he went to the theatre every night. He didn't have time to sit at home, watching television.
	ETHEL	Oh.

They hear someone snoring.

Sidney, what's that? I can hear something. Oh, look!

SIDNEY	Where?
ETHEL	Over there. There's a man over there, behind the newspaper. I think he's asleep.
SIDNEY	Oh, yes. He must be one of Shakespeare's family. He's probably Shakespeare's grandson.
ETHEL	Ooh!
SIDNEY	I'll just go and say 'Hello'.

He goes over to the man and shouts.

Hello!

	MAN	What? Eh? What's going on?
III	SIDNEY	Good morning.

MAN	Good mor – Who are you?
ETHEL	We're tourists.
MAN	Tourists?
SIDNEY	Yes.
ETHEL	It must be very interesting, living here.
MAN	Interesting? Living here? What are you talking about?
SIDNEY	Well, it must be interesting, living in a famous house like this.
MAN	Famous house?
ETHEL	Yes, there must be hundreds of people who want to visit Shakespeare's house.
MAN	Shakespeare's house? Look, there must be some mistake.
SIDNEY	This *is* Shakespeare's house, isn't it?
MAN	*This* is Number 34, Railway Avenue . . . and *I* live here!
ETHEL	Yes. You must be Shakespeare's grandson.
MAN	Shakespeare's grandson?
ETHEL	Yes.

IV

SIDNEY	Ethel! Look at this!
ETHEL	What is it?
SIDNEY	Look at it!
	He is holding an ashtray.
ETHEL	Ooh, Shakespeare's ashtray!
SIDNEY	Yes, William Shakespeare's ashtray! Mr Shakespeare, I would like to buy this ashtray as a souvenir of our visit to your grandfather's house.
MAN	For the last time, my name is not –
SIDNEY	I'll give you ten pounds for it.
MAN	Now listen . . . Ten pounds?
SIDNEY	All right then. Twenty pounds.
MAN	Twenty pounds for that ashtray?
ETHEL	Well, it *was* William Shakespeare's ashtray, wasn't it?
MAN	William Shakespeare's . . . Oh, yes, of course. William Shakespeare's ashtray.
	Sidney gives the man twenty pounds.
SIDNEY	Here you are. You're sure twenty pounds is enough . . .
MAN	Well . . .
SIDNEY	All right then. Twenty-five pounds.
	He gives the man another five pounds.
MAN	Thank you. And here's the ashtray.
	The man gives Sidney the ashtray.
SIDNEY	Thank you very much.
ETHEL	I hope we haven't disturbed you too much.
MAN	Not at all. I always enjoy meeting people who know such a lot about Shakespeare. Goodbye.
ETHEL	Goodbye.
	Ethel and Sidney leave.

Questions

I 1 How many tourists were there?
  2 Where were they?
  3 Why didn't Shakespeare use a typewriter?
II 4 Which tourist knew more about Shakespeare?
  5 Were the tourists alone in the room?
  6 Describe the man's reaction when he woke up.
III 7 Was the man Shakespeare's grandson?
IV 8 What did the tourists want to take home with them?
  9 Why did they want to take it home?
  10 Was the man still annoyed when they left?

Impossible!

Read the following 'life history' of Shakespeare and make comments on it.

> William Shakespeare was born in Tokyo in 1564 and died in 1697. He wrote his first play at the age of four. He worked as a garage mechanic before becoming a full-time playwright. He didn't leave his home-town until he was twenty-three. In 1584, he bought a car and drove to London. He then travelled widely round Europe, visiting Paris, Berlin, and Rome in the same week. He was a good friend of Charles Dickens and Winston Churchill.

Word Puzzle

Do you know where Shakespeare was born? Put the correct words in the vertical columns, and the letters in the box will spell the name of the town.
Read the complete text before you write the words.

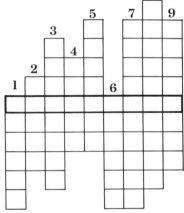

The man and the woman in the sketch were (3) . . . . Their names were (1) . . . . and (2) . . . . Shakespeare wrote a lot of (4) . . . . The woman thought that he wrote them on a (8) . . . . The man said that Shakespeare used a tape-recorder, and imagined him with a (7) . . . . in his hand. The man said that Shakespeare was too busy to watch television, because he went to the (5) . . . . every night. They thought the other man was Shakespeare's (9) . . . . They told him he was lucky to live in a (6) . . . . house.

Communicating

Are You Sure?

A In the sketch, Sidney seems to know a lot about Shakespeare. When someone speaks like this, you may want to make sure they know what they are talking about. These expressions are useful:

What makes you think so?	How do you know?
Are you sure?	That can't be true.

B When Sidney and Ethel talked about the typewriter, Sidney said 'That can't be Shakes-peare's typewriter.' But he did not give the right explanation. You could begin:

> That can't be Shakespeare's typewriter, because . . .

and continue:

> . . . Shakespeare lived 400 years ago.
> . . . typewriters weren't invented then.
> . . . typewriters are modern.

Practise in pairs, talking about the typewriter and the television.

In Your Own Words
Re-enact the sketch in your own words, without reading from the text. Do it in short sections. These words will remind you:

Writing

A Dialogue
After the two tourists had left, the man telephoned a friend. This is what the man (A) said. What did his friend (B) say?

A : Hello? Fred, is that you?
B : . . . .
A : I'm fine. You know, something really strange has just happened.
B : . . . .
A : Well, I woke up and found two tourists in my front room.
B : . . . .
A : Because they thought it was *Shakespeare's* house!
B : . . . .
A : No, I'm being serious. They wanted to buy a souvenir of their visit.
B : . . . .
A : Yes, I sold them an ashtray.
B : . . . .
A : Twenty-five pounds.
B : . . . .
A : I'm *not* joking. It's true!

What Do You Think?

Souvenirs
When you visit a famous monument or building – a cathedral, for example – you often find shops nearby, selling souvenirs. These are often badly-made, ugly, a horrible colour and very expensive.
Do you think the manufacture of souvenirs like this should be stopped?